We appreciate you working to renew interest in saving our California missions.

—Jean Hoffmann, Grand Secretary, and Alice Forbes, Grand President, Native Daughters of the Golden West

The authors, Pat Hunter and Janice Stevens, have beautifully crafted an extraordinary artistic and readable presentation of California Mission history. This work reflects the personal love and accurate understanding of the authors and captures the richness of California history, bringing a fresh view of the Franciscan Missions. *Remembering the California Missions*, offers the reader an appreciation, both that can be used as an introduction for young students coming to know history for the first time; or as a deepening resource to those still "young at heart" growing in their love and appreciation of the Missions and history of California. The authors have creatively amalgamated through their talent of art and history a resource that will enrich any library. This book will help to relive a history that has shaped California and continues to stir the soul of many through the rich spirituality and culture of our great State. Speaking as a Franciscan, and administrator of one of the California Missions, I enthusiastically endorse this work of Pat Hunter and Janice Stevens.

—Father Larry Gosselin, O.F.M., Guardian, Old Mission San Miguel

This beautifully written and illustrated book is a must read for anyone interested in California history. Two especially helpful features of this book are the Glossary and Bibliography. Many words, so common at that time, are no longer in usage today. The extensive Bibliography includes books, periodicals, brochures and electronic sources. This is a book for all ages, and it would be a fine addition for libraries and classrooms, as well as home collections.

—Dr. John Taylor, Fresno County Superintendent of Schools (Ret.)

Remembering The
CALIFORNIA MISSIONS

Paintings by Pat Hunter ∾ Text by Janice Stevens

Craven Street Books
Fresno, CA

Remembering the California Missions

© 2010 Pat Hunter and Janice Stevens. All rights reserved.

Published by Craven Street Books,
an imprint of Linden Publishing.
2006 S. Mary, Fresno, California, 93721
559-233-6633 / 800-345-4447
CravenStreetBooks.com

Craven Street Books is a trademark of Linden Publishing, Inc.

Craven Street Books titles may be purchased in quantity at special
discounts for educational, fund-raising, business, or promotional use.
Please contact Special Markets, Craven Street Books, at the
above address or at 559-233-6633.
To order another copy of this book, please call
1-800-345-4447

Craven Street Books project cadre:
James Goold, Carla Green, Doris Hall, John David Marion, Kent Sorsky
ISBN: 978-1-884995-64-4
135798642

Printed in China.

Library of Congress Cataloging-in-Publication Data on file.

Acknowledgments

With deep appreciation for their suggestions and contributions:

Margaret Barrett

Susan Bennett

Aileen and Gene Bos

Ron Branam

Florence and Ron Greilich

Joan Hall

Earlene Holguin

Dr. Burton James

Elizabeth Laval

Vic Maggi

Nadine Marsh

Bob and Kay Owens

Adriana Roe

Linda Scambray

Bill Secrest Jr.

Bill Secrest Sr.

Kent Sorsky

Richard Sorsky

Monica Stevens

Lidia Villane

The book designers: Jim Goold and Carla Green

Overleaf: Mission San Antonio de Padua on the Hunter Liggett military base

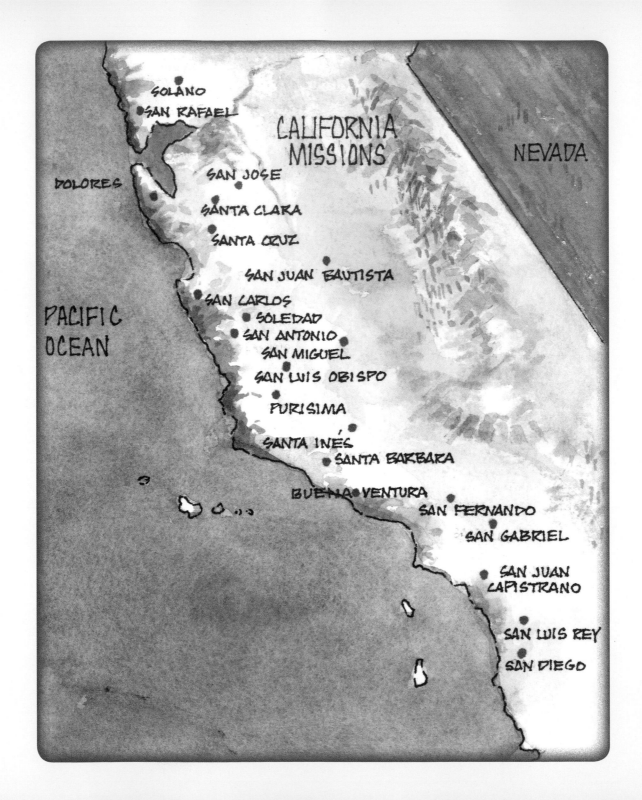

Table of Contents

Preface

THE MYSTIQUE OF the California missions has fascinated me since I was a teenager celebrating fiestas and family picnics at Mission San Antonio. This remote mission, originally located on the old El Camino Reál, was the scene of speculation, imagination, and wonderment for the early pioneers of California who forged the trail to civilization.

In later years, reading articles and hearing stories about decay and crumbling walls—symbols of the end of the mission era—brought these earlier memories back. At one point, Pat Hunter and I set out on a "mission run" to capture in watercolor the portraits of these once spectacular places. But life has a way of redirecting interests and priorities and, after gathering material for a few paintings, we abandoned the idea of a full set.

In 2008, after completing our book *William Saroyan: Places in Time*, Pat and I pondered what project to pursue next. We selected one and began our research. However, our publisher wasn't as enthused as we were over this particular subject and suggested we look into the California missions. We were delighted by the idea and immediately went to work, traveling up and down the old padres' trail to visit and research each mission. And, as quite often happens, one thing led to another. Previously unknown details and discoveries intensified our excitement, and old memories flooded back.

Today, most of the missions have been restored and recreated—some rebuilt from a single wall or two of ruins, others in replica—to teach the history that began more than 200 years ago. Pat and I hold a deep appreciation for the organizations and individuals who believed so strongly in the restoration and preservation of the rich heritage of California's missions, and backed words with deeds: the Native Daughters and Sons of the Golden West; Daughters and Sons of the American Revolution; women's clubs statewide; the Landmark League; the William Randolph Hearst Foundation; the California State Parks; the National Park Service; and especially the individual missions and their mission communities.

A small statue of Father Junípero Serra sits on a shelf in a china hutch in Pat's dining room. That image and a few Indian artifacts are heirlooms she received from her mother, who as a fourth grade teacher had used the items in teaching about the California missions, a course requirement for all fourth graders in California public schools. We offer the following pages not only as our own attempt at assisting in the preservation of this unique aspect of California's cultural history, but also as tribute to Pat's mother and to all fourth grade teachers, past and present, who have instilled a love of history in their students.

It is our hope that you, too, will immerse yourself in the bygone era illustrated in this book, and that in doing so you will come to appreciate the glory of the California missions. Perhaps you will even feel inclined to embark on your own journey of discovery—just as Pat and I did while visiting the missions sequentially, in the order of their founding, traveling the Kings Highway from the first mission, in Southern California, to the last mission, located in Northern California, the founding of which ended the Golden Age of the California missions.

—Janice Stevens, February 2010

Prologue: The California Missions

SPANISH INVOLVEMENT in Alta California (the present-day State of California) began in 1542, when explorer Juan Rodriguez Cabrillo was commissioned to discover new territory for the Spanish Crown in the New World. Cabrillo first sighted Alta California when he sailed into what is now San Diego Harbor. He continued his voyage up the California coast, but he decided the area was a forbidding wilderness, and abandoned any plan to claim Alta California for Spain.

The next Spanish explorer to visit Alta California was Sebastián Vizcaíno, who explored the country in 1602–1603. Vizcaíno enthusiastically described the Monterey Bay coast to the viceroy of New Spain. The viceroy ordered Vizcaíno to establish a settlement at Monterey Bay, but that plan was canceled in favor of exploring Japan.

Alta California's wealth remained untouched for 150 years, until Gaspár de Portolá led an expedition there in 1769, guided by Cabrillo's crude maps of the region. Portolá's orders were to provide a military presence to protect the territory; the far more daunting task of converting the native Indians to Christianity fell to Father Junípero Serra.

Serra was a highly respected and well-educated Franciscan priest born in Majorca, Spain, who had been serving in the missions of Baja California, Mexico. The Baja California missions had originally been established by the Society of Jesus, but in 1767 the king of Spain, disturbed by the Jesuit missionaries' increasingly independent empire, expelled the Jesuits from the missions. The king replaced the Jesuits with Franciscan fathers from the College of San Fernando in Mexico City, and Serra was appointed superior of the Baja California Missions.

When Portolá led his expedition into Alta California two years later in 1769, the Franciscan missionaries of Baja California were chosen to establish the "new missions" of Alta California. Father Serra, then 55 years old, who could command an assignment in universities as well as preach in large cathedrals, was ideally suited for this missionary task. Serra was dedicated not only to establishing Christianity throughout the New World, but also to educating the Indians to develop profitable communities within the mission system and forge a productive civilization in Alta California.

Serra accepted the office of president of the Franciscan missions of Alta California, leaving behind wealth and position to live frugally off the land.

The plan of Spanish colonization was for Father Serra to establish the first mission in San Diego, advance to Monterey, and then extend the chain of coastal missions into northern Alta California. Once the southern and northern coastal missions were self-sustaining, interior missions would be established in the territory's Central Valley.

Putting this plan into effect proved complicated. Father Serra and his missionaries contended with earthquakes and other natural disasters, as well as threats from the sometimes hostile Indians. Founding the missions required not only military strength, but ingenuity and perseverance.

The Spanish planned four initial expeditions into Alta California, two by sea and two by land. The first expedition ended in disaster. The first ship, the *San Carlos*, followed erroneous charts, sailed beyond the San Diego harbor, and had to turn around. The second ship, the *San Antonio*, arrived in San Diego before the *San Carlos* returned, but it had lost more than a third of its crew to scurvy. Their supply ship, which carried all of the expedition's supplies and provisions, was apparently lost at sea.

Despite setbacks and hardships, the Franciscans successfully established twenty-one missions in Alta California, from the founding of the first mission in 1769 to the last, San Francisco Solano, in 1823. At their height, the Franciscan missions stretched over a 2,000-mile range from Guadalajara in Baja California to San Francisco Bay in Alta California. Centuries later, these missions remain an enduring legacy of modern California.

1 ∽ El Camino Reál

THE **E**L **C**AMINO **R**EÁL, or The King's Highway, began in 1769 as a dusty footpath traveled by Gaspár de Portolá and the Franciscan padre, Junípero Serra, in their search for locations to found other missions, and ultimately stretched from Mission San Diego north to San Francisco de Solano.

The narrow pathway soon expanded, linking the missions, presidios, and pueblos, with each mission planned to be within a day's journey from the next. Meandering through alluvial plains and valleys, the route was traveled by soldiers, traders, and missionaries, and in time was widened into a stage road to accommodate mules, horses, and wagons. Eventually, the 700-mile-long El Camino Reál became, primarily, Highway 101, a major thoroughfare spanning the length of California. That route, however, did not follow the El Camino Reál exactly, as the original footpath traveled by Father Serra and other missionaries changed to accommodate the missions founded slightly off the main route. One of those routes includes Highway 82, where sections of the original El Camino Reál veer off from Highway 101.

In the beginning, the missionaries scattered mustard seed along the trail, which explains another name for the route: the Padres' Trail. Later, crosses burned into trees became identifying markers. An archeological discovery at Mission San Miguel revealed one of these tree barks, now displayed in the museum. It was common knowledge that the padres marked the trail in this fashion.

Living tree in Templeton with a cross carved in bark

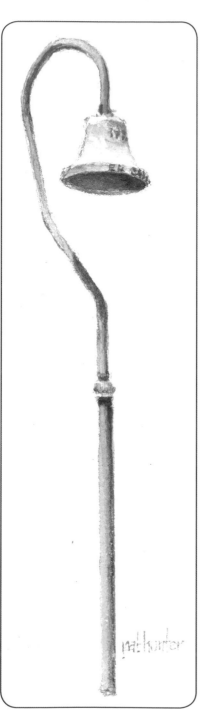

Guidepost bell marking the El Camino Reál

In 1892, Anna Pitcher, director of the Pasadena Art Exhibition Association, suggested marking the route of El Camino Reál in honor of the Franciscan's California missions. But it wasn't until 1902 that the Native Daughters of the Golden West and the California Federation of Women's Clubs, represented by Mrs. Armitage S. C. Forbes and Mrs. Caroline Olney, again addressed the proposal. The decision was finally made in 1906 by the Camino Reál Association to use guideposts to mark the trail.

Mrs. Forbes chose the image of a Franciscan walking stick holding a mission bell as the design. Manufactured at her husband's foundry, the first bell was of cast iron, weighed eighty-five pounds, and was supported by iron tubing eleven feet tall. This bell was dedicated at the Iglesia de Nuestra Señora Reina de Los Angeles, familiarly known as Plaza Church in Los Angeles, on August 15, 1906. Each bell is inscribed with the words "El Camino Reál 1769–1906" to indicate the founding of the first mission and the date of the dedication of the first bell.

Women's Club members had the vintage bell markers installed along the original El Camino Reál route, and the California State Automobile Association and the Automobile Club of Southern California maintained them from 1926 to 1931.

By 1913, the El Camino Reál had more than 450 bells spaced at one-mile distances, with one in front of each mission and historical site. In 1959, California State's Division of Highways took over the maintenance duties. Unfortunately, over time a number of the original bells were lost due to vandalism, theft, and road construction.

On August 15, 2006, to commemorate the placement of the first bell on the El Camino Reál, the descendants of the members of the California Federation of Women's Clubs and the Native Daughters of the Golden West gathered at the Plaza Church in Los Angeles to ring in the bells' second century. The following day, a *Los Angeles Times* article by Bob Pool reported:

> The ladies did the heavy lifting 100 years ago.
>
> Members of the two groups helped state officials unveil a replica of the 85-pound, cast-iron bell that pioneering women's organizations erected August 15, 1906, in downtown Los Angeles as the state's first road marker.
>
> Each has been cast from the original molds made 100 years ago by women's club member Mrs. Armitage C.E. [S.C.] Forbes, the mastermind of the civic coalition that created the original highway markers.
>
> A hands-on leader, Forbes herself poured molten metal into the bell-shaped forms in a corner of a foundry owned by her husband. She eventually created a business entity, California Bell Co., to manufacture them. Bearing the legend, 'El Camino Reál,' and the dates, '1769 & 1906,' each marker also had a small sign on its post showing the distance to the next town or mission.

Today, the California Bell Company, in conjunction with Caltrans, is replacing the missing bells on the El Camino Reál, and to date has installed 555 new bells between San Diego and Sonoma.

On December 29, 1963, the California State Park Commission, in cooperation with the Committee for El Camino Reál, placed a plaque at the San Diego Mission, which reads: "El Camino Reál. This plaque is placed on the 250th anniversary of the birth of California's apostle Padre Junípero Serra, O.F.M., to mark the southern terminus of El Camino Reál as Padre Serra knew it and helped to blaze it. 1713–November 24–1963. California Registered Historical Landmark No. 784." An identical plaque was placed to mark the northern terminus of El Camino Reál at Mission San Francisco de Asís (Mission Dolores).

The California State Park Commission, in cooperation with the Sonoma Parlor No. III, Native Sons of the Golden West, placed a plaque on July 14, 1963, at Mission San Francisco Solano marking the end of El Camino Reál (California Registered Historical Landmark No. 3). It read: "On July 4, 1823, Padre José Altimira founded this northernmost of California's Franciscan Missions. In 1834, secularization orders were carried out by military commandant Mariano G. Vallejo. San Francisco Solano became a parish church serving the pueblo and Sonoma Valley until sold in 1881. This plaque replaces one originally dedicated by the Historic Landmark Committee, Native Sons of the Golden West, 1926."

Diverging east of Highway 101, a remnant of the original El Camino Reál meanders north of the cemetery at Mission San Juan Bautista. The narrow dusty trail borders

Highway 101—El Camino Reál today

fields of crops reminiscent of the days of industrious missionaries and neophyte (Indian convert) laborers. The familiar guideposts punctuated with sporadic yellow mustard on the Padres' Trail is strongly suggestive of that momentous period of history that began with the founding of the California missions. Father Junípero Serra's vision continues to resonate in the twenty-first century.

Remnant of the original El Camino Reál—Padres' Trail

2 ∿ Mission San Diego de Alcalá

AFTER **F**ATHER **S**ERRA received his assignment and position as president of the Franciscan missions of California, he consulted with Visitador General Don José de Gálvez to discuss Spain's royal plans for founding the missions in Alta California. The ambitious plans included founding the first mission and presidio in Port San Diego, followed by the next mission in Monterey, a considerable distance up the coast of Alta California.

After arriving in Mexico, Father Serra left on one of two land expeditions from Loreto, Mexico, for San Diego on March 28, 1769. On the journey, he stopped and founded Mission San Fernando Rey de España de Velicata in Baja California on May 14, 1769, before traveling 150 miles north to the port of San Diego in Alta California.

Reaching San Diego, Father Serra, along with Governor Gaspár de Portolá, united with the Franciscans and soldiers who had arrived two days earlier traveling by ship. While Governor de Portolá journeyed northward on a narrow dirt path (the initial segment of the El Camino Reál) to locate Monterey for the second mission in California, Father Serra remained, working closely with fellow fathers Juan Viscaíno, Francisco Gomez, and Fernando Parron. They chose a site overlooking the San Diego Bay adjacent to the Indian village of Cosoy. After constructing huts and shelters out of brush, on July 16, 1769, Father Serra raised the wooden cross where the future chapel would stand, said the Mass, and officially established Mission San Diego de Alcalá (named in honor of Saint Didacus of Alcalá), the mother of the great California missions.

After the mission was underway, Father Serra left it in the care of Fathers Gomez and Parron and traveled up the coast to meet with Governor de Portolá for the founding of the Monterey mission.

Unfortunately, the original site of California's first mission proved to be inadequate to produce the agriculture necessary to sustain the mission and the soldiers at the nearby presidio. Father Luis Jayme, who succeeded the other fathers, requested permission to move the mission complex. The viceroy approved, and the San Diego mission relocated six miles northeast of the presidio near the Nipaguay Indian village. By December 1774, the church, council, and rectory buildings had been constructed, as well as thirteen buildings to house the neophytes (Indian converts) who provided the labor for the community.

Mission San Diego de Alcalá

The mission grew rapidly, with more than five hundred Indians baptized, but Mission San Diego de Alcalá was to earn a tragic distinction. It was the only mission of the twenty-one to be attacked by its neophytes. The Indians resented the harsh treatment given them by presidio soldiers, and Indian leaders were threatened by the spiritual influence of the mission. The Indians revolted, set fire to the mission, and stole ornaments, clothing, and anything else of value while the missionaries slept. Although most of the missionaries were able to escape, Father Jayme deliberately walked into the midst of the attacking Indians to offer peace. He was brutally killed in the attack and thus became California's first martyr.

Father Serra returned to San Diego from Monterey to rebuild the mission and to meticulously rewrite his records, which had been destroyed in the Indian uprising. By October 1776, reconstruction began on a large church, with stone foundations, enclosed within a high adobe wall to better withstand another Indian attack.

However, an earthquake in 1803 caused considerable damage to the church, necessitating the building of a third. Even before this church was finished, another earthquake destroyed it. The padres, undaunted, began again and devised the idea of buttresses to support the buildings. The supporting wooden beams reinforced the adobe construction and offered stability against the threat of additional earthquake damage.

The mission prospered with 1,405 converts and land holdings of 50,000 acres, consisting of vineyards and crops of barley, wheat, corn, and beans. Orchards and vegetable gardens thrived close to the mission. Livestock included 20,000 sheep, 10,000 cattle, and 1,250 horses.

Father Serra's room at Mission San Diego

Bell tower with five original bells given by the Viceroy, 1796

Sadly, the encroachment of civilization on the mission and the political upheaval after Mexico won its independence from Spain and occupied Alta California introduced an ensuing fifteen-year period of decline for Mission San Diego. From 1820 to 1830, the fathers lost much of their authority over the mission lands. José M. Echeandía, the first Mexican governor to rule over Alta California, introduced the Act of Secularization on August 17, 1833. Under this act, the government seized the mission land and sold it as private property to Mexican settlers in Alta California.

I. Brent Eagen, in his book *A History of Mission Basilica San Diego de Alcalá, The First Church of California, Founded by the Venerable Junípero Serra, July 16, 1769,* wrote:

In answer to the pressure exerted by Californians interested in obtaining Mission lands, Mexico began to appropriate Mission properties. Mission San Diego de Alcalá was given over to Santiago Arguello for services rendered the government in the year 1846. The last Franciscan priest in service of the Mission, Padre Vincente

Oliva, retired to San Juan Capistrano in that same year.

In 1847 the famous U. S. Cavalry took over occupation of the Mission grounds. Soldiers were stationed here periodically for the next fifteen years.

Eagen observed that there are conflicting reports describing the usage of the mission during those years. One such report discusses the destruction of the mission buildings to accommodate army occupation. However, the *Bartlett Report* of 1854 describes the adobe buildings as being well preserved and kept "in good repair."

On May 23, 1862, President Abraham Lincoln ordered the mission's twenty-two acres returned to the Catholic Church for religious use. Sadly, the demise of Mission San Diego could not be prevented and in less than twenty years all that remained was the *fachada*, or front wall.

Interestingly, "The mission dam, built six miles up the river in 1816, outlasted the mission that it served by several decades. Its stored water was brought to the mission by miles of aqueduct. It stood unbreached until a flood burst it open. As late as 1930, a large segment still stood," writes Paul C. Johnson, supervising editor of *The California Missions: A Pictorial History*.

Archeological excavations have revealed the original layout and plans of California's first mission and offer insight into the mission way of life. Today the Mission San Diego de Alcalá stands proudly, the recipient of careful restoration. Offset from the plain adobe front of the church, the bell tower—or *campanario*—rises above the top of the building and houses five distinct bells; these include the approximately 1200-pound Mater

Doloros bell, cast in 1894 from four original bells the viceroy gave to Mission San Diego in 1796.

In the bicentennial year of 1976, Pope Paul VI declared the mission church a minor basilica, and it continues today to serve the Catholic parishioners in the community.

Santa Ysabel, Asistencia to Mission San Diego de Alcalá

Santa Ysabel Asistencia, founded by Father Fernando Martin on September 20, 1818, was intended to serve the 250 neophytes who lived too far from Mission San Diego to receive spiritual instruction and training. The padres petitioned the governor for permission to establish this outpost to the mission, but were refused. Nevertheless, the padres constructed a small temporary chapel, followed by permanent adobe buildings, including a granary, neophyte housing, and a chapel with a cemetery nearby. The submission grew quickly, and by 1822 the neophyte population had nearly doubled. Unfortunately, secularization in the 1830s caused the *asistencia* to be sold. The church fell into such disrepair that the Indians used a brush arbor for services conducted by visiting priests or the village chieftain.

"Only two bells, bought by the Indians themselves for six burro loads of barley and wheat, remained for several years, hanging from a crude framework, until they vanished in 1926," writes Kenneth C. Adams in *California Missions*.

Stories abound about how these bells disappeared and their whereabouts today, and occasional sightings offer hope that some might be returned to the mission, but so far those hopes have been in vain.

The Santa Ysabel Asistencia site was originally registered on April 3, 1940, as California Registered Historical Landmark No. 369. On September 26, 1987, a plaque was placed at the site by the State Department of Parks and Recreation in cooperation with the Roman Catholic Diocese of San Diego, the Santa Ysabel Tribal Council, and Squibob Chapter #1853, E Clampus Vitus. The plaque reads: "Father Fernando Martin celebrated the first Mass on September 20, 1818, at a site nearby, an outpost of Mission San Diego. By 1822 Santa Ysabel had a chapel, cemetery, granary, many houses, and 450 neophytes. After secularization in the 1830s, priestly visits were rare. Tradition asserts that services have been held here since 1818, under armadas erected against one wall after the roof caved in. The present chapel was built in 1924."

Restoration of the present 1924 stucco chapel was supervised by Father Edmond La Pointe, a Canadian-born priest of the Sons of the Sacred Heart, who served the area for 29 years and who is buried in the cemetery next to the church.

3 ～ Mission San Carlos Borromeo de Carmelo

AFTER THE FOUNDING of Mission San Diego, Gaspár de Portolá set out on a land expedition to find Monterey Bay in order to establish a presidio to provide a military presence on the coast. At the same time, Father Junípero Serra set sail on the *San Antonio* to found the second mission.

The parties rendezvoused in Monterey and agreed to formally establish Mission San Carlos de Borromeo on June 3, 1770, on the grounds of what would become the Monterey Presidio. Mission San Carlos de Borromeo was named for Saint Charles Borromeo, who was born in Italy in 1538, the first great leader of the Counter-Reformation.

Father Serra erected a cross under an oak tree—purportedly the same oak tree where explorer Sebastián Viscaíno held Mass in 1602—and Governor de Portolá took formal possession of Monterey Bay and its surrounding lands for King Carlos III of Spain.

Not long after founding Mission San Carlos, Father Serra realized the location would be unsuitable for a permanent site, because of the lack of available drinking water and the shortage of Indians to evangelize. In May 1771, Father Serra moved the mission several miles inland to its present location on the Carmel River and, as president of the California missions, established his headquarters at Mission San Carlos Borromeo de Carmelo (which would later become known as the Carmel Mission).

Father Serra lived simply, as was expected of the Franciscan friars, 100 yards from the church in a small cell with a single blanket on a cot of boards, a table with a candlestick on it, a chair, and a chest. His collection of thirty books would eventually grow to more than 600, including *Father Serra's Bible*, and become known as the first library in California.

Courtyard at Carmel Mission

Mission San Carlos Borromeo de Carmelo

Father Serra's cell while serving as president of the California missions

A few years after building a small wooden chapel, soldiers' quarters, and storehouses, Father Serra made grand plans for the construction of the Mission San Carlos de Borromeo church, but he did not live to see his vision realized. Shortly before he died, Father Serra instructed his close friend, Father Francisco Palóu, "When the stone church is built, you may place me where you will."

Upon Father Serra's death on August 28, 1784, his close friend, Father Palóu, acquired the presidency of the mission chain. But due to ill health, he soon relinquished the position to Father Fermín Francisco de Lasuén, who would go on to found as many missions as Father Serra did.

In 1791, Father Lasuén commissioned Manuel Ruíz, a master mason, to design and build the Mission San Carlos Borromeo de Carmelo church, using stone quarried from the area, an unusual departure from the adobe construction of other missions, but specifically requested by Father Serra.

Ruíz incorporated Moorish architecture in his design for the church, with two distinctive asymmetrical bell towers and a large star window over the front doorway. The larger tower, with a Moorish-style dome, holds nine bells, mostly still original, accessible by an outside stairway to the belfry. The smaller, simpler tower holds just one bell. A slightly irregularly shaped quadrangle encloses the workshops and living quarters.

The lush gardens offer beauty and serenity, housing olive trees and meticulously groomed plants and shrubs. Fountains repeat the Moorish architectural influence of the church, and carvings of the Dominicans' and Franciscans' coats of arms, as well as statues of their founders, Saint Dominic and Saint Francis, are imbedded in the stone wall surrounding the courtyard.

Father Serra, who had been buried in the small adobe church, was then entombed in the large stone church. Years later, in an attempt to preserve Father Serra's earthly remains as well as his legacy, funds were raised to build a glorious sarcophagus for his grave. But when it was completed in 1924, the parishioners successfully protested, wanting the Father's remains to be left intact, buried under the altar of the church in the fittingly simple manner Father Serra would have desired.

In 1803, Father Lasuén passed away and was buried next to his friend in the massive stone church. The headquarters of the California missions was then transferred to Santa Bárbara.

A frightening occurrence took place in November 1818, when two ships belonging to the notorious pirate Hypolite Bouchard came within sight of the mission. The governor and the mission community fled inland while the 400 looters from the ships ransacked and burned Monterey; however, it is unknown if the pirates reached the mission grounds, which were later found to be unharmed.

Mexico's secularization act impacted Mission Carmel, as it had Mission San Diego. The mission's lands were confiscated and sold and its buildings were left to decay. The abandoned mission's roof gave way, but the stone walls stood for more than thirty years. In 1884, restoration funds were acquired to repair the roof, but it wasn't until the 1930s that the restoration of Carmel Mission began in earnest.

Beginning in 1931, under the capable and dedicated hands of Harry Downie and his associates, restoration brought back the glory of Mission Carmel that secularization, earthquakes, and neglect had

nearly destroyed. The San Carlos Borromeo de Carmelo Mission was elevated to a minor basilica in 1961. Today, the mission is a California classic landmark, in frequent use as a parish and for the public's visitation.

On the Monterey presidio grounds, San Carlos Borromeo de Monterey was designated a Royal Presidio

Side entrance stairway to the choir loft

Royal Presidio Chapel

Chapel because, as the only church in the capital, attendees included Spanish governors and provincial and foreign dignitaries. Designed and constructed by Manuel Ruíz from 1791 to 1795, the current presidio chapel, which replaced the original wood chapel built in 1770, clearly resembles Mission San Carlos Borromeo de Carmelo.

The Royal Presidio Chapel has been in continuous use since 1794, with visiting friars serving as pastors, until it became an active parish church. It is the only remaining presidio chapel. In 1850, the chapel was designated the first cathedral in California and was dedicated as a National Landmark in 1961. It is also considered to be the oldest stone building in California.

4 ∿ Mission San Antonio de Padua

AFTER THE ESTABLISHMENT of Mission San Carlos Borromeo de Carmelo, Father Serra traveled south on the El Camino Reál from Monterey with a small party of soldiers, neophytes, and two other Franciscan padres, Fathers Buenaventura Sitjar and Miguel Pieras, to found his third mission in the Central Coast region, slightly inland from the El Camino Reál. Father Serra sought the San Antonio Valley, recommend to him by Governor Portolá, who had camped there on his way north from San Diego in search of Monterey Bay.

East of the Santa Lucia Mountains, upon entering the Valley of the Oaks, the party set up camp near a small stream that Father Serra christened Rio de San Antonio. A large brass bell taken from a packing mule's back was hung on the branch of an oak tree to begin Mass, the first order of business. In his enthusiasm for the site, Father Serra rang the bell and ecstatically proclaimed, "Hear, oh Gentiles! Come; oh come to the holy church of God! Come, oh come and receive the Faith of Christ!"

When questioned by Father Pieras as to why he would say that with no Indians to address, Father Serra offered a simple reply (as noted by mission historian Father Zephyrin Engelhardt in *California Missions*, by author Kenneth C. Adams): "O Father Miguel, let me give vent to my heart's desires; for I would that these bells were heard all over the world, or at least by all pagan people who live in this sierra."

Setting out a large wooden cross with a makeshift altar under a brushwood shelter, Father Serra founded Mission San Antonio de Padua on July 14, 1771, in honor of Saint Anthony from Portugal, renowned for being a miracle worker, for defending the poor, and for his preaching.

Upon the timely appearance of a single Indian woman, Father Serra believed his mission would be fruitful. "I trust in God and into his favor of San Antonio that this mission will become a great settlement of many Christians, because we see here what has not been observed in any of the other missions founded hitherto, that at the first holy Mass, the first fruit from paganism has been present. He will surely not fail to communicate to his tribesmen what he has seen," Serra said, according to Father Engelhardt.

Father Serra's words proved to be prophetic as the Indians did come, bearing acorns and other gifts, and the mission population grew to more than 1,800 neophytes.

Construction of the mission compound progressed rapidly, with the padres overseeing the labor provided by the Salinan Indians. With the proximity of the Rio San Antonio to the mission site, the first aqueduct and reservoirs in California were constructed, along with irrigation ditches to carry water to the fields, and a water-powered mill for grinding grain.

The mission prospered, with ample production of wheat and thousands of cattle and sheep. The Salinan Indians were renowned for their basket weaving, and the vineyards offered quality wines.

Father Buenaventura Sitjar, who served for thirty-seven years overseeing the development of the mission, also authored a 400-page book of the vocabulary and grammar of the Telame language spoken by the Indians. Through that accomplishment, the Indians learned to read and understand the foundations of the Christian faith they observed in Father Serra and the other padres.

With the change from Spanish to Mexican rule, the large demand for food, money, and clothing to care for the military threatened the existence of the mission. On November 12, 1834, politicians under the authority

Ruins of the reservoir from a sophisticated water system

Mission San Antonio de Padua

of Commissioner Manuel Crespo, in enforcement of the Secularization Act, seized the mission property.

Although the Indian population had declined over the years as a result of exposure to European diseases, the remaining Indians were allowed to stay at the mission. But without the protection of the missionaries, they were mistreated and often became addicted to liquor. Many fled to their former lives in the mountains to live off seeds and game, as they had before their conversion to Christianity.

Adams details this sorrowful change in *California Missions*: "On December 31, 1835, Father Mercado, reporting on conditions at the once happy and prosperous Mission San Antonio, wrote: 'so numerous are the Indians who wander about as fugitives or as vagabonds that one cannot prudently name an estimate.' Only a few years before, these natives had been happy and industrious under the regime of the padres."

Before long, the thousands of cattle, sheep, and rare golden Palomino horses were gone, and the vast orchards, vineyards, and productive grain fields were left unattended.

In May 1845, Governor Pío Pico attempted to sell the forsaken mission for the equivalent of $8,269, but it had been looted and damaged to such an extent that no bidders came forth. Even under the care of Franciscan Reverend Doroteo Ambris, who superintended the property from 1851 to 1882, the mission's remote location continued to make it an easy target for ransackers and plunderers.

The United States conquered Alta California in 1846, but didn't officially acquire the region until the United States and Mexico signed the Treaty of Guadalupe Hidalgo of 1848, which ended the Mexican War. After the death of Franciscan Father Ambris, the mission was again abandoned, leading to even greater deterioration. The red tiles used to roof the buildings—the first such in the mission chain and forerunners to the mission theme predominant in California architecture—were stolen and sold by an antique dealer to roof a railroad station. Other buildings were demolished and their timber taken.

On May 31, 1863, Abraham Lincoln decreed that Mission San Antonio was to be returned to the hierarchy of the Catholic Church.

In 1903, Joseph R. Knowland, a state senator and future congressman, formed the California Historic Landmarks League. He later served as president of the Native Sons of the Golden West in 1909. Promoting the combined goal of the two preservation groups, he toured California to recruit interest and funding to restore Mission San Antonio de Padua to its former glory.

Although work was hampered by the devastating earthquake of 1906 (which did extensive damage to many of the missions) and additional damage suffered in 1948, restoration efforts were again attempted. Through combined effort, the California Landmarks League, the Native Daughters and Sons of the Golden West, the Franciscan fathers of California, and the William Randolph Hearst Foundation, with a grant of $50,000, completed the extensive restoration of the mission.

Harry Downie, who had earned an exemplary reputation for his restoration efforts on the Carmel Mission, supervised the labor provided by some of the descendants of the original neophyte builders of the mission.

One remaining bell of the three bells that hung in the *companario* in 1821, called the Osquila, continues to ring out to an active parish church, where Franciscan friars have lived and served the mission since 1948. A statue of Saint Anthony in the church sanctuary reminds the parishioners of the mission's namesake, who was buried in Padua, Italy.

Seemingly ageless oak trees reflect the time of the mission's founding on July 14, 1771, and in the spring, wild flowers carpet the valley under the Santa Lucia Mountains.

The mission is accessible through the military compound of Hunter Liggett, an arrangement which protects it from an encroaching population.

Padres' garden

5 ∾ Mission San Gabriel Archángel

ACCOMPANIED BY SOLDIERS for protection and to guard the mules laden with goods and supplies, Father Angel Fernandez de la Somera and Father Pedro Benito Cambón, appointed by Father Serra, sought a site for a fourth California mission near the Rio de Nombre de Jesus de los Temblores, or River of Earthquakes, now known as the Santa Ana River. But concerned about the threat of earthquakes, the group continued on, eventually crossing the San Gabriel River into the San Miguel Valley.

Upon the fathers' arrival at their desired location, Tongva Indians threatened them. Legend has it that, fearing they would be killed in the fight, one of the fathers pulled out a canvas painting of Our Lady of Sorrows and showed it to the Indians. The reaction was astounding. Bows and arrows were lowered, and the two Indian chiefs removed their necklaces of beads from around their necks and laid them on the ground before the painting to offer their respect and as a token of peace. The fathers placed a cross of sapling, gathered from the riverbanks, and celebrated the Mass, founding Mission San Gabriel Archángel on September 8, 1771.

Fascinated by the pageantry of the Mass, the Tongva Indians, known for their spirituality, quickly converted and were baptized the second day after the mission's founding. The revered 300-year-old painting of Our Lady of Sorrows is displayed in the old mission church.

In spite of the goodwill between the fathers and the Indians, the soldiers, whose purpose was to assist and protect the mission, used their authority to abuse the Indians. In one incident, a soldier's assault against an Indian chieftain's wife led to a battle that killed the chief, thus destroying the friendship and trust between the missionaries and the Indians.

Fertile lands produced crops of corn, wheat, barley, and beans, as well as a large variety of fruits. Herds of cattle, sheep, and goats roamed the ranges. Abundant flower and vegetable gardens were protected by large cactus, used as a natural barrier to fence in the areas.

But it wasn't long before the flooding from the river caused a move to higher ground in 1775. Although the first buildings were made from the saplings, willows, and reeds abundant on the riverbanks, buildings of adobe bricks were used for the new construction.

The unique architectural design, unlike any of the other missions, was provided by Father Antonio Cruzado from Cordova, Spain, and reflects some of the Moorish influence of the cathedral of Cordova. The entrance to the

Mission San Gabriel Archángel

mission church is on a sidewall under capped buttresses seven feet thick, with the rest of the walls four to five feet thick. The windows are long and narrow. The roof is vaulted. An outside, hard-burned, brick-over-stone staircase leading to the choir loft was the only access until 1908, when inside stairs were constructed. The stone, brick, and mortar church is considered to be the oldest structure of its kind south of Monterey.

Original door on the side entrance to the church

Outside stone staircase leading to the choir loft

The baptistry's domed ceiling, floors, and walls have been well preserved, and the hand-hammered copper baptismal font and silver baptismal shell brought by the fathers from Spain in 1771 continue to be used by the parish.

In 1993, after the 1987 Whittier Narrows Earthquake, a cedar shingle roof was installed on the recommendation of the State Office of Historic Preservation.

The process of restoration provides an understanding of the vast system managed by the padres and produced by the labor provided by the Tongva Indians. Excavations in the two quadrangles reveal the ruins from the kitchen and open fireplaces. A fifteen-foot-deep water cistern, the remains of soap and tallow vats for making candles and soaps, clay pipes from the aqueduct, and a tannery all suggest the productivity and self-sufficiency of the mission. Two olive trees date back to 1860, and the grapevine in the quadrangle dates to about 1910.

Oldest cemetery in Los Angeles, featuring a 100-year-old grapevine

Vineyards thrived in the climate of southern California, and by the 1820s the mission boasted the largest winery in California. Tongva Indians stomped the juices from the grapes with their bare feet, and the wine ran down the slope of the floor to a trough where it was gathered and stored in wine barrels.

Under the guidance of Father José Maria Zalvidea, San Gabriel Mission earned the reputation as the "Pride of all Missions," because of the wealth it gleaned from agriculture, wine, olive oil, and the other products it created.

The San Gabriel Mission padres' hospitality was well known, and the mission became a gathering place for traders and travelers to do business as well as receive food and shelter. Besides the El Camino Reál, two other historical trails converge at the San Gabriel Mission. In

1774, Juan Bautista de Anza forged what is now known as the Juan Bautista de Anza National Historic Trail when he traveled from Tubac, Mexico to the San Gabriel Mission.

Years later, in 1829–1830, Antonio Armijo traveled from Santa Fe, New Mexico, with sixty men and pack mules carrying woolen goods to San Gabriel Mission, where he traded the goods for additional horses and mules before returning to Santa Fe. Thus the Old Spanish Trail, as it became known, opened trade and communication between the provinces of California and New Mexico.

With the Mexican government's passage of the Secularization Act, the mission ranches were confiscated.

A few years later, in 1846, under the administration of California Governor Pío Pico, the property was traded to two Americans to settle creditors' debt.

The United States declared this title illegal, and in 1855, under President James Buchanan, the mission was returned to the church; however, the Franciscan friars had left in August 1852, leaving the mission to secular clergy.

In 1908, the Missionary Order of the Sons of the Immaculate Heart of Mary—also known as the Claretian Missionaries, named for their founder, Saint Anthony Mary Claret—took possession of and maintained their headquarters at the San Gabriel Mission.

Six bells of varying sizes, and ranging in dates from 1795 to 1830, are encased in openings in the campanile, each designed for the specific size of the bell it contains. Of significance are two bells assumed to have been cast by Paul Ruelas as a gift from the king of Spain on behalf of Father Serra. The largest bell in the campanile "… has rung the Angelus over the countryside for over a century. Its clear tone could be heard in the Pueblo of Los Angeles, eight miles away. Weighing at least a ton, it hangs from a crown-shaped top, symbol of a royal bell. Dated: 1830," notes supervising editor Paul C. Johnson in *The California Missions.*

In the mission cemetery, Campo Santo, which is the oldest cemetery in Los Angeles (except for a Chumash burial ground in Malibu) a large crucifix stands in memorial to the more than six thousand Tongva Indians who succumbed to cholera and smallpox epidemics. Franciscan and Claretian missionaries and parishioners are also buried in this cemetery. The cemetery outside

Bells of varying sizes and shapes dating from 1795–1830

the quadrangle adjacent to the mission began to be used in the early 1800s.

Today, the San Gabriel Mission, with its lush gardens and well-preserved and restored buildings rich in mission history, continues to serve the community as the "Pride of all the Missions."

Nuestra Señora La Reina de Los Angeles Asistencia, or La Plaza Church

Nuestra Señora La Reina de Los Angeles Asistencia, which means "Our Lady Queen of the Angels," was founded in 1781 to provide an *asistencia*, or sub-mission outpost, to Mission San Gabriel. "The relationship of San Gabriel with the City of Los Angeles dates from the arrival of forty-four *pobladores* (early settlers of Los Angeles), accompanied by a company of soldiers, who crossed the Rio Portiuncula and founded the Pueblo de Nuestra Señora de Los Angeles de Porciuncula. This historic event took place on September 4, 1781, just a decade after the establishment of the mission," writes Monsignor Frances J. Weber in his book *The California Missions*.

Three years after the *asistencia's* founding, its first church—La Plaza

Church—was completed.

"The mission Native Americans who originally worked on the construction of the church were paid a coin known as a Spanish real each day, which amounted to about 12.5 cents," writes author James Osborne in *Missions of Southern California*.

Legend has it that the first California Yankee Don, Joseph (Juan José) Chapman, a former cohort of the

Nuestra Señora La Reina de Los Angeles Asistencia (La Plaza Church)—the oldest landmark in Los Angeles

notorious pirate Hypolite Bouchard, built the La Plaza Church. However, one theory is that he was not a pirate, but instead a Yankee shipbuilder who had been shanghaied by pirates and then caught while jumping ship during Bouchard's attack on the Ortega Rancho near Santa Barbara in 1818. Saved by the beautiful daughter of the Ortega family, Chapman was taken to Rancho San Antonio by Los Angeles mayor Don Antonio Maria Lugo, where he was put on parole and gained a reputation as a miracle worker because of his skilled artistry. Credited with building the first gristmill in California in Santa Ynez, he is especially noted for his work on the old Plaza Church. After the cornerstone was laid, it was eight more years before the construction was dedicated on December 8, 1822.

Chapman, after obtaining amnesty from the king, was baptized as Juan José in 1822, and he married Maria de Guadalupe Ortega at the San Buenaventura Mission. He bought a home and land near San Gabriel Mission in 1824 and continued to aid the missionaries at the mission.

The La Plaza Church underwent major reconstruction in 1841 and 1842 after receiving damage from a leaky roof, and was remodeled again in 1861, at which time the adobe front was replaced with brick, and the original flat brea roof was replaced with shingles. The *campanario* has niches for three bells.

Padres from Mission San Gabriel visited the *asistencia* to offer Mass and provide other spiritual instruction, in addition to offering food and supplies to both the settlers and the Indians in the area.

After the Secularization Act, Nuestra Señora La Reina de Los Angeles Asistencia (La Plaza Church) became a parish church and is considered to be one of the oldest parish churches on the West Coast. It is located across the street from Union Station and Olvera Street, the oldest street in Los Angeles.

In 1906, Mrs. Armitage S.C. Forbes selected La Plaza Church as the location to dedicate the first bell along the El Camino Reál, to honor the perseverance of the Franciscan pioneer fathers in their effort to settle and Christianize California.

San Bernardino Asistencia

The San Bernardino Asistencia, established in 1830, is located on Barton Road in Redlands. In *Missions of Southern California*, a postcard reads, "It was part of Mission San Gabriel's Rancho San Bernardino and had fallen into ruins until 1925 when the San Bernardino Historical and Landmark Society began its restoration."

The *campanario* is separate from the *asistencia* and resembles the *campanario* on the San Antonio de Pala Asistencia associated with Mission San Luis Rey.

The small chapel at San Bernardino, built in the 1830s, was restored in the 1930s and dedicated as California Historic Landmark #42 in 1960.

6 ∾ Mission San Luis Obispo de Tolosa

GASPÁR DE PORTOLÁ DISCOVERED and named La Cañada de los Osos, or the Valley of the Bears, on September 7–8, 1769, during his famed expedition from San Diego in search of Monterey, and he enthusiastically recommended the site as ideal for a mission community. Father Serra founded Mission San Luis Obispo de Tolosa, the fifth mission, on September 1, 1772, and dedicated it to Saint Louis, bishop of Toulouse, France. Before returning to mission headquarters in Monterey, Father Serra appointed Father José Cavaller to serve as the mission's administrator.

Cavaller quickly won the friendship of the local Chumash Indians, who were grateful to the soldiers for killing the savage bears so prevalent in the valley. The Indians offered seeds and other foods to trade for bear meat, and they willingly aided the missionaries in building the original mission structures, using native materials of poles, tree boughs, and other plant material in the construction.

But after hostile Indians from the Central Valley set at least three fires before 1774, destroying these primitive structures, the fathers devised a way to recreate and refine the red tiles first introduced by Mission San Antonio de Padua. The rounded roof tiles were fire-resistant and thus offered some protection for the plaster-covered adobe walls and stone-and-mortar floors of the new structures. Living quarters for the missionaries, a *convento* wing, storerooms, soldiers' barracks, and mills made up the traditional quadrangle.

The restored mission still displays the round pillars with square foundations that surround the porches in the courtyard, a detail not used in any of the other missions. Two bells that were made in Peru by Manuel Vargas in

Sculpture of bear and child in front of the mission

Three garden bells

tiles for use by other missions. The mission also gained a reputation for the high-quality cloth woven by the neophytes from the mission's sheep. The Indians became adept at weaving heavy serapes, as well as clothing to trade or share with other missions.

The 1810 Mexican War for Independence resulted in even harsher demands on the self-reliant missions, and in spite of Mission San Luis Obispo's notable accomplishments, Father Luis Martínez and the mission community, which provided for the military, often lacked provisions for themselves. Nevertheless, in spite of the stresses of having to accommodate the politicos, Father Martínez's good humor was legendary. One incident involved Father Martínez parading all the barnyard animals before an important visiting general.

However, his criticism of the governor also made Father Martínez many enemies. In 1830, after thirty-four years of service, he was banished from Mission San Luis Obispo. Father Luis Gil y Taboada was appointed to take Father Martinez's place in 1830, but he died in 1833 and was buried in the floor in front of the sanctuary. The mission declined rapidly over the next ten years. The last remaining Franciscan, Father Ramon Abella, died in 1842. Finally, in 1845, Governor Pío Pico sold the mission to Scott, Wilson & Company for $510.

Following the American occupation of California in 1846, United States President James Buchanan declared the sale illegal and returned Mission San Luis Obispo to the Catholic Church in 1859.

Restoration, beginning in the 1870s, added a New England-style clapboard belfry over the exterior adobe walls.

1818, along with another recast from broken bell parts in 1878, still hang in arched openings of the belfry.

After Father Cavaller's death in 1788, Mission San Luis Obispo prospered under the guidance of Father Miguel Giribet, who was appointed senior missionary in 1790, and Father Luis Antonio Martínez, who was appointed to be Father Giribet's assistant in 1798. By 1800, under Father Martínez's supervision, a granary, weaving room, and adobe houses were constructed. Mission San Luis Obispo produced wine, olive oil, fruits, and vegetables, besides producing and marketing the red

Mission San Luis Obispo de Tolosa

Wooden floors covered the *mezcla*, and shingles replaced the rounded clay tiles.

In 1933, however, Father John Harnett began an ambitious project of tearing down the modernized structures and restoring the mission to its original architectural design. By the late 1940s, the original walls and floors were restored, and the wooden siding and tall steeple had been removed. Under Father Harnett's supervision, the interior was restored to reveal the earlier large beamed ceiling. The vestibule and bell tower were rebuilt, and the bells rehung.

In 1948, Harry Downie finished the restoration work begun by Father Harnett, using funds provided, in part, through a grant from the William Randolph Hearst Foundation.

Although little remains of the original exterior of the mission, the interior of the church has been well preserved and reflects the 200-year history of the mission. The baptismal font, with the adjacent statue of Saint Louis, continues to be used by the parish church.

Referred to as "The City with a Mission," the city of San Luis Obispo celebrates the founding of Mission San Luis Obispo each year in the town plaza in front of the mission.

Santa Margarita Asistencia

On August 20, 1769, Father Juan Crespí noted the location of what would become the Santa Margarita Asistencia on his journey to Monterey. Almost twenty years later, Mission San Luis Obispo established the Santa Margarita Asistencia, northeast of the mission proper. The primary purpose of the

Indian dwellings on Santa Margarita Ranch

asistencia was to provide a mission community to feed, care for, and convert the Indians who were unable to travel to the main mission. Traditionally, the *asistencia* did not have a resident priest, but was self-sufficient in all other ways. Growing crops, maintaining granaries for storage, and other aspects of mission life were the same. The outpost would also provide a place to aid the neophytes afflicted with diseases introduced by the European settlers.

During its prime, the Santa Margarita Asistencia provided a refuge for the missionaries fleeing the notorious pirate Bouchard after his attack on Monterey.

Nothing remains today of Santa Margarita Asistencia but ruins of the former storehouse and chapel. The ruins are enclosed in a large barn, with cracked adobe and stone ruins visible from the inside. The outpost is on private property, but the owners hold occasional community events during which the public is invited to visit the grounds.

Ruins of Santa Margarita Asistencia wall

Mission San Francisco de Asís

7 ∾ Mission San Francisco de Asís (Mission Dolores)

To DEFEND ALTA California from the threat of attack and colonization by other European powers, the viceroy of New Spain, Antonio Maria Bucareli, commissioned Captain Juan Bautista de Anza to recruit soldiers and their families to build a presidio and a mission in the location of the huge San Francisco bay earlier discovered by General Portolá, who thought it large enough to accommodate all the ships in Spain.

"The first object of the expedition is to conduct troops for the protection of the missions which it is decided to establish at the Port of San Francisco. Nothing is of such interest as the accomplishment of this for subsequent plans," Viceroy Bucareli wrote in a letter personally delivered to Father Serra, as recorded by historian Father Zephyrin Engelhardt, O.F.M., in his book, *The Missions and Missionaries of California, San Francisco or Mission Dolores.*

Mission San Francisco de Asís was the sixth mission founded under Father Serra's direction. Fathers Francisco Palóu and Pedro Cambón, along with expedition leader Lieutenant José Joaquin Moraga, founded Mission Dolores (its familiar name, based on the nearby rivulet called Arroyo de los Dolores) on June 29, 1776, in honor

Garden sculpture of Father Serra in cemetery

Chapel at the Presidio of San Francisco

of Saint Francis of Assísi, the founder of the Franciscan order.

Barracks and housing were soon ready, and Father Palóu celebrated the Mass at the Presidio of San Francisco on July 28. After a headquarters, a warehouse, and a chapel were completed, a dedication Mass was held at the Presidio Chapel on September 17, 1776.

Ships, including the *San Carlos*, brought in supplies from Mexico, and sailors worked with the fathers to construct the mission.

The roughly constructed mud-covered wooden mission chapel, with a roof made from tules, was richly decorated with banners and pennants from the *San Carlos*. Ringing bells, booming cannons, musketry, and fireworks launched from the ship contributed to the formal dedication of the mission on October 9, 1776. The noise and activity of the fireworks and rockets frightened the Indians away.

In subsequent years, more than 28,000 Indian baptisms

took place at the mission, but an epidemic of measles killed a number of Indians, and as a result, many fearful neophytes fled from the mission and what they perceived to be evil spirits. The mission buildings themselves were inadequate to house the ill, so to prevent as many runaway Indians as possible an *asistencia* was founded in San Rafael a few miles farther north. But the graves of five thousand Indians buried in the mission cemetery are testament to the severity of the diseases and the loss of Indian lives.

The mission church was completed in 1791 and is considered to be the oldest intact church of the twenty-one missions. The church is 114 feet long by 22 feet wide, with decorated buttresses lending structural support to the four-feet-thick adobe walls. The original redwood logs connected with rawhide support the tile roof. Four Doric columns support the exterior balcony.

The quadrangle consisted of living quarters for the padres and neophytes, workshops and storage areas, and a 150-foot-long granary. The neophyte women were renowned for tanning hides and making soap and tallow, as well as other products. Although located inland and not actually on the shoreline, the location of Mission Dolores was ideal for use as a shipping center, and it was used by several other missions as well to ship products to Spain and to England.

In 1810, the Mexican War of Independence from Spain set into motion the decline of Mission Dolores. "The process of removing the material, economic, and commercial operations (sometimes called temporalities) of the missions from the control of the Franciscans is called 'secularization.' The missions were not intended

Basilica built in 1918 to the right of the original mission church

to be permanent organizations. The plan was for the Indian villages surrounding the missions to be turned into self-governing townships within ten years of their establishment," wrote the Mission San Francisco de Asís curator, Brother Guire Cleary, in his book *Mission Dolores: The Gift of St. Francis.*

San Francisco Presidio today: view from Chrissy Field with the Presidio on the left and the Golden Gate Bridge behind

By 1834, the lands and possessions of Mission Dolores were confiscated, and the remaining Indians abandoned the mission.

The American acquisition of California took place in 1846, and the mission property was taken over by Gold Rush enthusiasts. "It was a sleepy isolated community

when the Gold Rush struck it like a cyclone. Because of its remoteness from the center of town, the neighborhood became a center for high jinks, and people flocked to the area to enjoy the horse racing, gambling, and tavern life that erupted here," wrote Paul C. Johnson in *The California Missions*. Johnson also noted that one of the mission buildings was even converted into the Mansion Hotel, a popular tavern noted for its "exhilarating milk punch."

Mission Dolores was returned to the Roman Catholic Church upon President James Buchanan's decree of 1858. But some of the adobe buildings were still leased out to private enterprise, and the quadrangle lands were sold to allow for the development of the San Francisco Mission District.

By 1876, a hundred years after Mission Dolores's founding, the population had outgrown the small mission chapel, and a new brick Victorian church was constructed to serve the parishioners. Although the small mission chapel came through the famous earthquake and ensuing fires of 1906 unscathed, all of the buildings surrounding it were destroyed. Even the large Victorian church was so structurally damaged that it had to be demolished.

Builders erected a new stone church beside the mission in 1918, after waiting out a halt in construction caused by World War I.

During preparations for the 1926 sesquicentennial celebration of the founding of Mission Dolores, the designers who were remodeling the 1918 stone church were influenced by the predominantly Spanish Baroque architecture featured in the San Diego-Panama-California Exposition of 1915. Upon its completion, Pope Pius XII designated the church a minor basilica, making it an honorary Church of the Pope.

Adjacent to the majestic basilica, Mission Dolores offers a simple contrast, remaining relatively untouched since 1791. It is the oldest standing building in San Francisco.

"Though dwarfed by the overwhelming mass of the Mission Dolores Basilica to the north, the mission chapel and its bosky cemetery present a picture of unassuming serenity. Basilica status was granted in 1952 because of [the] historic importance of the mission," writes Johnson.

8 ∾ Mission San Juan Capistrano

MISSION SAN JUAN CAPISTRANO is legendary for the yearly migration of *Las Golondrinas*, or cliff swallows, which travel six thousand miles from Argentina to the mission walls, where they build their nests of mud and saliva.

Bells ring out on the day of their return in celebration, and the ringing of the bells has become as legendary as the return of the swallows themselves. Four bells hang in the restored campanile that replaced the earlier bell tower, and the largest bell is inscribed with the name of each padre who served the mission.

Fathers Fermín de Lasuén of San Carlos Borromeo and Gregorio Amurrio of San Luis Obispo were assigned by Father Serra to establish Mission San Juan Capistrano. Their first attempt was the simple placement of a lonely cross on October 30, 1775, by Father Lasuén, who had arrived ahead of Father Amurrio. But with news of an Indian massacre at San Diego, the mission soldiers immediately set out to help, and the fathers and a bodyguard followed, after burying the two mission bells. After quelling the uprising, the two padres lingered in San Diego, until Father Serra received word from Viceroy Bucareli to return to San Juan Capistrano and complete the founding.

Upon Father Serra's return, October 30–31, 1776, he found the cross, dug up the bells, hung them on a tree, and established Mission San Juan Capistrano, the "Jewel of the

Swallow nests in the mission eaves

Missions." It was the third mission on the El Camino Reál and the seventh mission to be founded. He then rang out the bells to alert the Indians of the missionaries' return.

The Indians worked together with the missionaries to construct an arbor and altar, under which Father Serra celebrated High Mass, officially founding Mission San Juan Capistrano on November 1, 1776.

The idyllic landscape overlooking rolling hills and valleys that stretch to the sea must have pleased Father Serra. The location was fifty-eight miles from what would five years later become Los Angeles.

As San Juan Capistrano Mission grew and prospered, the Indians were housed in adobe buildings and taught the skills of weaving, carpentry, and agriculture.

In 1797, the fathers decided to build the largest and most elaborate church of all the mission buildings. Isidor Aguilar from Caliacon, Mexico, a skilled stonemason, was commissioned to design the Great Stone Church, and his plan was to build the church in the shape of a Latin cross. The church was not finished until 1806. History records posted at the time of secularization indicate that more than two thousand Indians had lived at the mission, and men, women, and children had worked together to create the church. The men carried the heavy stones from the quarry; the women and children brought back pebbles and small stones in their hands and aprons. Limestone mortar held the sandstone together.

The vault and the long, stately arches of sandstone and limestone mortar, seen in the surviving stonework, are reminiscent of ancient Roman and Greek ruins.

Although one of the most populous missions, Mission San Juan Capistrano, as with many other missions, was ravaged time and again by earthquakes. The earthquake of December 8, 1812, was particularly destructive, destroying the 120-foot-high bell tower. The roof and walls of the massive stone church collapsed, killing forty adult Indians and two boys, with only six people surviving the destruction. The devastating earthquake spared only the back wall, which continued to demonstrate the intricate design of skilled craftsman.

The Great Stone Church vault

Mission San Juan Capistrano

Original wall ruins of the Great Stone Church

Father Zephyrin Engelhardt, in *The Missions and Missionaries of California, San Juan Capistrano Mission,* reports that:

Fathers Francisco Suñer and José Barona, the two missionaries then in charge, reported the calamity as follows: "On the eight day of this month (December) consecrated to the Most Pure Conception of the Most Holy Virgin, a terrible earthquake occurred while the first holy Mass was being celebrated, which was about (the figure is torn out) in the morning. In a moment it completely destroyed the new church built of masonry (cal y canto). It required more than nine years to construct it, but it lasted no more than six years and three months to the day; for it was blessed on September 8, [7], 1806. The tower tottered twice. At the second shock, it fell on the portal and bore this down, causing the concrete roof to cave in as far as the transept exclusively."

The fathers had no desire to rebuild the mission church until 1814. But another discouraging event occurred in 1818, when Hypolite Bouchard, the pirate who invaded and seized Monterey, attacked San Juan Capistrano, burning buildings and looting the mission.

By 1821, the growing discontent between the military, the civil government, and the missionaries took another toll on Mission San Juan Capistrano. The mission was forced to contribute finances and products to the Mexican government, which added to the resentment felt in the mission community.

When José M. Echeandía—the first native Mexican to govern California—ordered the fathers at Mission San Juan Capistrano to swear allegiance to the Mexican government, they refused to do so. Governor Echeandía became determined to destroy the California missions, and began to emancipate the California mission Indians. Governor Figueroa, who succeeded Echeandía, continued to emancipate the San Juan Capistrano Indians, and he also confiscated the mission's lands, giving some to the natives and the rest to his friends. Although a majordomo was assigned to the mission, a padre named Father Zalvidea stayed with the mission in order to be close to the remaining neophytes.

By 1841, after the turmoil of changing governmental regimes, the Indians were gone and their lands had been distributed to the settlers. The government proclaimed the mission complex a pueblo, and within a year the last missionary to serve Mission San Juan Capistrano, Father Zalvidea, was gone, leaving the mission with no priest for four years.

On December 4, 1845, the ultimate blow came with the sale of the mission at public auction. Governor Pío Pico sold the mission to his brother-in-law, John (Don Juan) Forster, and to Forster's business partner, James McKinley.

On July 7, 1846, the Americans seized California and raised the American flag at Monterey.

Engelhardt notes in his book: "The United States Land Commission, appointed to examine the land cases in California, on December 18, 1855, declared Pico's sale of the mission property illegal. Likewise, the United States District Court declared that Pico had no authority to sell the missions. Accordingly, the churches, the adjacent dwellings, the cemeteries, the orchards, gardens, and vineyards, which in Spanish Law, recognized by the Land

Serra Chapel, the only chapel to still exist where Father Serra conducted Mass

Commission and the United States Court, were regarded as belonging to the Catholic Church and needed for the

Parish basilica today

maintenance of Divine Worship, were by United States Patent restored to the Catholic Church...."

On March 18, 1865, President Lincoln ordered San Juan Capistrano to be returned to the Catholic Church.

Sixty years passed, during which time the mission fell into further decay, until 1895 when Charles F. Lummis and the Landmarks Club began restoration work. Serra Chapel, built in 1782, is the only remaining original building, and it is of historical significance as it is the only chapel left today where Father Serra conducted Mass. It is reputed to be one of the oldest structures in the state.

Of note, a large baroque *retablo*, a large ornamental screen behind the altar, adorns the chapel. Although not original to San Juan Capistrano, it is believed to be three hundred years old. The piece was sent from Barcelona, Spain, in 1906, to be used by the Archdiocese of Los Angeles, but was stored until brought out in 1924 and trimmed to fit the Serra Chapel.

Beginning under the guidance of Father St. John O'Sullivan in 1910, subsequent archeological discoveries and restoration have revealed buildings that once surrounded the odd-shaped quadrangle. Museum displays show the diverse cultures represented at Mission San Juan Capistrano: the American Indians and their ways, the Spaniards who first possessed California and established the chain of California missions, and the Mexican ranchos. Museum tours and reenactment events feature workshops, which illustrate soap and candle making, furnaces for cooking and metallurgy, and vats for tanning hides, a major export for the mission community. Fiestas to celebrate the return of the swallows are always planned for March 19, Saint Joseph's Day.

9 ～ Mission Santa Clara de Asís

IN ORDER TO PROTECT against the threat of enemy attack on the northern coastline of Alta California, Viceroy Antonio Maria Bucareli authorized two mission settlements to be established near the port of San Francisco. After Mission Dolores was founded a year earlier, Father Tomás de la Peña founded Mission Santa Clara de Asís on January 12, 1777, near the river Rio de Nuestra Señora de Guadalupe, a site which had been selected earlier by Juan Bautista de Anza. Father de la Peña planted the cross and with the aid of Lieutenant José Joaquin Moraga, his soldiers, and their families, built a crude brush arbor in order to conduct Mass. Mission Santa Clara de Asís was the first to be named in honor of a woman, Saint Claire of Assisi, the founder of the Poor Clares Order of nuns.

Relief sculpture detail on Mission Santa Clara church

With the arrival two weeks later of Father José Murguía, who brought supplies and livestock from Monterey, construction of the mission began.

Unfortunately, flooding in November 1779 destroyed the original buildings, so Father Peña began construction on a new church in November 1781. That, too, was destroyed by floods. A third church, designed by Father Murguía, was considered to be the most imposing edifice in California at the time. Father Murguía passed away, four days before the dedication of his last effort, on May 15, 1784.

Father Serra, *Presidente* of the Missions, officiated at the event, the last one of its kind that he supervised. Feeble,

Large wooden cross on the college campus

and believing his time was nearing an end, Father Serra had been traveling the Kings Highway, making a farewell tour of his beloved Franciscan missions. Two little Indian altar boys at Mission San Gabriel told their priests, "The Old Father wants to die."

But Father Serra, despite his more than seventy years, was determined to arrive in time for Mission Santa Clara de Asís's dedication.

Father Serra's vigor and enthusiasm in delivering the High Mass surprised Father Palóu, who thought Serra was well enough to continue on after the dedication. But Father Serra, recognizing his frailty, expressed his desire to return to Mission San Carlos.

From the outset, continual confrontations with the local Indians threatened the survival of Mission Santa Clara, and Father Peña was finally compelled to request aid from the military.

However, it was not just the Indians who caused turmoil for Santa Clara; the settlers in the nearby small pueblo of San José were another problem, and disputes over the water rights to the Guadalupe River were frequent.

Father Magin de Catalá, who had succeeded Father Murguía at Mission Santa Clara, was able to resolve the issue by establishing the Alameda, a part of the El Camino Reál, in 1799. The four-mile road, lined with rows of black willow planted by the Indians, was a thoroughfare designed to link the communities, encourage church attendance, and lessen tensions between the two groups.

Whereas both floods and earthquakes took a toll on the California missions, the northern missions fared better than the southern missions during the devastating earthquake

Mission Santa Clara de Asís

Church arcade on the north side of the mission

of 1812. However, the large adobe church, which had survived thirty-four years, fell during the earthquake of 1818. The fifth church building was constructed in 1825.

With Mexican Independence from Spain, the growth and prosperity of the Santa Clara mission, whose crops were second only to Mission San Gabriel's in production, soon came to an end. In 1836, under secularization, the mission lands and property were confiscated, and the San José pueblo took the mission church for their parish.

The lands were returned to the Catholic Church after the American occupation, and in 1851 Bishop Joseph Alemany of San Francisco deeded what remained of the mission property to the Jesuit Order to establish Santa Clara College, the first college in California.

Unfortunately, in 1926, fire destroyed the mission church, and in addition to the collapse of the tower, the bells were damaged as well.

With just remnants of adobe left after the fire, the church was reconstructed, enlarged, and rededicated on May 13, 1928. It continues to operate as a parish church. The reconstruction largely duplicates the original mission church. A small fragment of the original large wooden cross that Lieutenant Moraga and Father de la Peña erected is encased inside a cross of concrete. Another cross, a reproduction of the original design, stands in front of Mission Santa Clara, now located on the University of Santa Clara campus. Both the Mission Santa Clara de Asís and the university continue under the Jesuit Order, a testament to their endurance.

10 ∾ Mission San Buenaventura

FATHER **S**ERRA PLANTED the cross and celebrated Mass on Easter Sunday, March 31, 1782, at La Playa de la Canal de Santa Bárbara, or Santa Barbara Channel beach. He was accompanied by Father Pedro Cambón, Governor Felipe de Neve, and a full military escort and their families, along with supplies and livestock from Mission San Gabriel. Mission San Buenaventura, the last mission founded under Father Serra's rule as President of the California Franciscan missions, and one of six Father Serra personally founded, is located on El Camino Reál, about seventy miles from Los Angeles, in present-day downtown Ventura.

Once construction was under way, Father Serra returned to his headquarters in Monterey and sent Fathers Francisco Dumetz and Vicente de Santa Maria to manage the new mission. The friendly Chumash Indians, who numbered more than 20,000 in the villages along the channel, willingly aided the missionaries in constructing the buildings.

The first mission was reported to have been destroyed by fire after ten years, and construction began again around 1793 of a new church composed of stone masonry. Living quarters for the neophytes, a tannery, and granaries were constructed as well. In 1809, the stone church was completed, and High Mass was celebrated on September 9 of that year.

Three years later, the earthquake of 1812 and resulting tsunami activity devastated the church. Again, it underwent repairs and reconstruction, including a new stone buttress on the left side of the front door to add strength to the

Moorish-Gothic detail above garden-side door

Distant view from Mission Street

6½-foot-thick adobe brick and stone walls. Also unique to this mission is the Moorish-Gothic-inspired arch above the garden-side door, with two stone pilasters on either side. Above this side door, two curved lines are symbolic of the two rivers that flow on each side of the mission.

The Mission San Buenaventura church has a triangular symbol on the façade, perhaps in reference to the Holy Trinity (God, the Father; God, the Son; and God, the Holy Spirit). The tall, asymmetrical tower, with the upper sections not centered on the lower sections, consists of a *campanario* of five bells. Two of the bells date back to 1781, and another dates to 1825.

Although the quadrangle was smaller than those of other missions, it still accommodated living quarters for the fathers and the military, as well as dormitories, workshops, and gardens. Neophyte Chumash Indians lived outside the quadrangle in conical huts made from willow trees.

Mission San Buenaventura's agriculture, consisting of orchards, vineyards, and grain fields, extended from the mission to the Pacific Ocean, and tropical fruits such as bananas, pears, figs, and coconuts grew in abundance. The mission thrived under the guidance of Father José Señan, who was President of the Franciscans in California, and was known for its sophisticated reservoir and aqueduct system, including a seven-mile-long stone-and-mortar canal that covered the distance from the mission to the ocean.

Mission San Buenaventura

However, the continued demands for food and clothing to support the military, which no longer received assistance from Mexico due to the revolt against Spain, put an added burden on the Indians' labor.

Father Señan believed that supporting the Santa Bárbara presidio was too much for the mission Indians and protested the demands of the presidio captain, José de la Guerra. Tensions came to a head when a group of Mojave Indians came to visit Father Señan. Corporal Rufino Leiva disliked the Mojaves fraternizing with their Chumash Indian cousins, and he questioned their motives. He consequently imprisoned them in spite of the Señan's request for their release. One of the Mojave Indians was punished, and the others angrily broke out and killed Corporal Leiva. The resulting battle resulted in the deaths of both Indians and soldiers. The incident created animosity between the Spanish and the Mojaves, who for years continued to revenge the loss of life at San Buenaventura and attack settlers.

In June 1836, Mission San Buenaventura was secularized and the mission lands were divided and sold, although in 1862 the church and some of the land was returned.

In 1893, Father Ciprian Rubio, while trying to update the mission complex, removed all of the buildings, changed the Indian designs, and replaced the Mexican altar.

The mission was restored to its original appearance in 1957, but the orchards, vineyards, and fields have long since disappeared. Today, nothing remains of the original mission buildings except for the reconstructed mission church and garden. Whereas once the mission was part of a square quadrangle with an enclosed patio, stores and business have absorbed the land, leaving just one side open for a walkway. Directly across the street from Mission San Buenaventura, a beautiful fountain plaza offers a peaceful and serene respite for visitors.

11 ∾ Mission Santa Bárbara

IN 1769 GASPÁR DE PORTOLÁ, traveling with Father Juan Crespí, reached Santa Bárbara by a land route and recommended the site to Father Serra.

Two years later, in 1771, Father Serra, traveling from San Gabriel, reached Santa Bárbara and also saw the potential for a mission and presidio. He obtained permission from the viceroy of Mexico, who ordered Governor Felipe de Neve to proceed. However, Governor Neve was becoming increasingly suspicious of the power of the missions and thwarted the founding of the Santa Bárbara mission, as well as any further mission founding. Neve was ordered back to Mexico in 1782 and Governor Pedro Fages was appointed to replace him.

The local Chumash Indians, including a few Yokuts (also called Yanonalits, after the local chief's name), were friendly and worked with the soldiers in building barracks and other buildings for the presidio. On Father Serra's last trip to visit all the missions before his death, he administered the holy Sacrament of Confirmation in Santa Bárbara at the presidio chapel. Unfortunately, Father Serra died in 1784, before seeing his plan for Mission Santa Bárbara realized. Father Fermín Lasuén raised the cross and blessed the site for the new mission on December 4, 1786, but the formal dedication was postponed until December 16, 1786, when Governor Fages could attend.

Father Lasuén assigned Fathers Cristobal Oramas and Antonio Paterna of Mission San Luis Obispo to the Santa Bárbara Mission, after being assured that the San Fernando College in Mexico would send six more padres to the California missions. The Franciscan college had previously been concerned about the future of the missions in California and had been reluctant to send missionaries to the area.

The two newly arrived priests lived at the nearby presidio while overseeing the construction of the mission church and the quadrangle of adobe buildings. The first church was crudely built of logs, reeds, thatch, and mud in 1787, but two years later a church made of adobe, with a tile roof, replaced it. Just four years after that, yet another church building was under construction. It was completed in 1794 and lasted until the devastating 1812 earthquake. Finally, the present church was built, with construction spanning the years 1815 to 1820.

Each church was built on the existing site. The fourteen Stations of the Cross were given to the mission in 1797 and have been an integral part of the church nave to this day.

Mission Santa Bárbara, "Queen of the Missions," is located on a hill, with its majestic demeanor overlooking the bay. The mission, with its world-famous 87-feet-tall twin bell towers, resembles an ancient Latin temple in pre-Christian Rome. The design was influenced by the Spanish edition of *The Six Books of Architecture*, composed by Vitruvius Pollio in 27 B.C. and published in Madrid in 1787. The book was brought to California by the Franciscans and is carefully preserved in the mission library. The blend of neoclassical influences with mission-style architecture is unique to the California missions, and restoration efforts have carefully preserved the original design.

The church was built using native yellow sandstone with crushed seashells in lime mortar, and the walls are six-feet-thick and supported by square stone buttresses. Statues encased on the church front represent Faith, Hope, and Charity. The mission roof consists of traditional red tiles.

An advanced water system, a reservoir made of masonry, and a large fountain, selected by Father Serra because of its location near the Pedragoso Creek, were constructed in 1806–1808. Two stone basins and dams were built on the creek, and aqueducts carried the water to the mission, some of which went through a filtering system to provide clean drinking water. Overflow from the beautiful Moorish-style fountain fell into the *lavanderia*, a stone laundry basin where Indians did their washing. A large gargoyle of a mountain lion still sits at the entrance to the *lavanderia* and is reputed to be the oldest and largest Chumash Indian stone sculpture in California.

Original gristmill and covered reservoir

Mission Santa Bárbara

Despite the abundance of living quarters, food, and clothing provided for the Chumash, and the opportunity to learn trade and agriculture, the Indians at Mission Santa Bárbara were resentful of the mission's support of the military. The Indian revolt of February 21, 1824, at Mission Santa Inés affected Santa Bárbara as well. Soldiers from the Santa Bárbara Presidio were sent to quell the uprising, and after the death of two neophytes and three soldiers, the Indians escaped to the mountains. Captain José de la Guerra, the presidio commandant, dispatched a force to pursue them. "A skirmish ensued in which four Indians were killed. Later, Father [Antonio] Ripoll and

Entrance to *lavenderia*: oldest and largest Chumash sculpture in California

Father [Vicente] Sarría accompanied an expedition into the mountains and persuaded the frightened fugitives to return to the mission, but not before four defenseless natives had been slain by soldiers on the mission grounds and the adobe homes of the neophytes looted," reports author Kenneth C. Adams in *California Missions.*

By July 15, 1833, Governor José Figueroa ordered emancipation for the mission Indians, and a year later he ordered mission secularization. The Franciscan missions were confiscated and their lands and possessions were seized. Because of the influence of both the last *presidente* of the missions, Father Narciso Durán, and the first bishop of California, Francisco Garcia Diego, Santa Bárbara fared much better than did the rest of the missions. Sadly, both men died in 1846, at which time Mission Santa Bárbara was sold to Richard S. Den for $7,500.

The new ownership was short-lived, however. The United States took possession of California in 1846, and a number of historical figures are recorded in mission records as having visited the mission, including Commodore R. F.

Stockton and Colonel John C. Frémont. On May 31, 1850, according to Adams in *California Missions*, "The Very Rev. Joseph Sadoc Alemany, Provincial of the Dominicans, was named by the Pope to be first Bishop of Monterey with jurisdiction over all of California."

It was due to the efforts of Alemany that Rome agreed to the founding of an ecclesiastical college at Santa Bárbara, and that it was appointed the mission of the Franciscans to found the college in 1853.

President Lincoln formally returned Santa Bárbara Mission to the Church on March 18, 1865.

Although the Queen of the Missions is the only mission in the California chain to have twin bell towers, both were added to the structure at a much later time. One tower was built in 1820, and the second was built eleven years later. The Franciscans have remained a presence at Santa Bárbara Mission since its inception in 1786, and the mission candles have burned continuously. With its classic European style, the Santa Bárbara Mission is a striking landmark in this coastal town.

12 ∾ Mission La Purísima Concepción

THE CHOSEN SITE FOR the eleventh mission, south of the Santa Ynez River, was a wide-open valley which offered ideal conditions for agriculture and for a successful mission community. La Purísima Concepción de Maria Santisima, "The Immaculate Conception of the Most Blessed Virgin Mary," was founded by Father Fermín Lasuén on December 8, 1787.

Father Zephyrin Engelhardt, O.F.M., in his work, *Mission La Concepción Purísima De Maria Santisima,* notes Father Lasuén's words recorded on the title page of the baptismal register:

> Book I of Baptisms of the Mission of the Most Pure Conception of the Most Holy Virgin Mary, Mother of God, and Our Lady, which was founded in the plain of the Rio Santa Rosa, on the site called by its natives, Algsacupi, at the expense of the Catholic King of Spain, Don Carlos III, (God protect him), by the Religious of the Apostolic College of the Propagation of the Faith of San Fernando de Mexico to whom his Majesty confided the Conversion and the Administration of this whole new California. It was commenced on … Saturday the 8th of the month of December 1787. On this day I, the undersigned *Presidente* of these Missions, blessed water and with it the place and a large Cross, which we venerated and planted ….

Soldiers from the Santa Bárbara Presidio provided labor, with the aid of the friendly converted Chumash Indians, to build the mission complex.

By 1802, a large adobe church, padres' quarters, residences for the soldiers and their families and for the married neophytes, as well as dormitories for unmarried women, were constructed using adobe and stone.

Fathers and neophytes toiled in the fields and handled the livestock, their efforts paying off in an increasingly profitable mission community under the guidance of Father Mariano Payéras, who served the mission for nineteen years, from 1804 to 1823. During his service at Mission La Purísima, Father Payéras also served as President of the California missions for four years, at which time the mission government was moved from Mission Carmel to Mission La Purísima.

In El Año del Temblor, the year of the 1812 earthquake, devastation afflicted many of the California missions, and La Purísima was not spared. The earthquake reportedly lasted four minutes and destroyed the church walls. A second quake, following shortly afterward, crumbled the rest of the buildings. "Then, like a wicked after thought, the hillside [at the] back of the mission opened a great crack, to let torrents of water flood the site, bringing complete devastation. Adobe,

Mission La Purísima Concepción

Original tallow vat used by the Chumash Indians

Working tirelessly and using man-made materials common to the missions—adobe, tule branches, clay tiles for roofing, and animal hides—the mission community built another large mission complex. The immediate concern was to provide shelter, and the residences were constructed with buttresses of stone supporting the 4 ½-foot-thick adobe walls. Warehouses for storing soap, tallow, and hides, a blacksmith shop and mill, and weaving and pottery rooms were all constructed. A sophisticated system composed of aqueducts, reservoirs, and clay pipes transported water from springs in the nearby hills. Sand and charcoal filtered the water for domestic use.

However, droughts and fires began to chip away at the hard-won prosperity. The Mexican revolt against Spain in 1821 affected the mission as well, creating the obligation to provide food, supplies, and payment to the soldiers.

When Father Payéras died in 1823, tensions intensified between the government, the missionaries, and the remaining Indians. By 1824, an Indian revolt was inevitable. Angry over mistreatment by the soldiers they were supporting, and hearing of even more abuse of the Indians at Mission Santa Inéz, the La Purísima neophytes took possession of the mission. Adding to existing walls and fortifications, they created a protected, fort-like structure and turned cannons on the soldiers, defending the mission and holding it for a month.

The governor, upon hearing of this uprising, sent reinforcements from the Monterey Presidio. Finally, Father Antonio Rodriguez offered a white flag of truce, and the skirmish ended. But the penalty paid by the Indians for their revolt was costly not only in terms of lives lost during

complete devastation. Adobe, tiles, tools, stock, and stores all disintegrated or floated on a sea of horror," wrote Paul C. Johnson, supervising editor of *The California Missions*.

Undaunted, the missionaries, burdened by the needs of the thousand neophytes now without food or shelter, asked and received permission to rebuild the mission on another site north of the Santa Ynez River and four miles northeast of the original mission location, in the "Canyon of the Watercress." El Camino Reál passed through the canyon, which made the new location even more accessible to trade and to visitors along the trail.

the fight, but in the punishment meted out by the military, which condemned seven Indians to death and imprisoned a dozen or more who were believed to have incited the revolt.

With Governor José Figueroa imposed secularization in 1834, the ruin of La Purísima was inevitable. By 1845, Governor Pío Pico, who succeeded José Figueroa, by illegal decree demanded the sale of the mission at auction to the highest bidder. The mission was sold for $1,100 to a man from Los Angeles: Jonathan (Don Juan) Temple.

This sale would be reversed in 1851. "The whole transaction of Pío Pico and his subservient legislators regarding the mission property was declared null and void by the U. S. Land Commission and by the U.S. Court, on the ground that Pico had no authority to sell the lands of the Missions," according to Father Engelhardt.

Not much remained of the original mission after years of neglect, except for a few wall ruins and pillars, when in the 1930s the National Park Service, utilizing a team of archeologists, engineers, historians, and architects, rediscovered the structure.

With the aid of the California Conservation Corps, who provided major reconstruction assistance from 1934 to 1941, the entire mission complex was rebuilt, using as many authentic tools and materials as possible. The mission and its lands were gifted to the state as the La Purísima Mission State Historic Park, and it is considered to have had the most elaborate restoration of all the missions. Today, the mission covers an expanse of 966 acres, including nine completely reconstructed buildings.

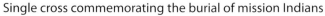

Single cross commemorating the burial of mission Indians

However, four miles southwest in the town of Lompoc lie the almost forgotten ruins of Mission Vieja, the original La Purísima Mission, which was destroyed in the December 1812 earthquake. Now, with some ruins accessible by public trail and others under private ownership, remnants of this first mission are revealed in the patio flooring of a residential chamber, and in stone walls scattered along the expanse of what had been the mission grounds. Undeveloped land, with remains of the adobe doorway to the Mission Vieja Church and aqueduct, stand in isolation nearly 200 years later.

Ruins of Mission Vieja, the original La Purísima Mission

13 ∿ Mission Santa Cruz

FATHER JUNÍPERO SERRA'S good friend and biographer, Father Francisco Palóu, highly recommended a site for the twelfth mission close by the San Lorenzo River in the city of Santa Cruz, a decision later endorsed by the viceroy and Father Matías Noriega in 1789. Two years later the cross was raised and the Mass said at the new site by Father Fermín Lasuén on August 28, 1791.

"However, Father Lasuén was not to be present at the dedication of the new mission," writes Kenneth C. Adams in *California Missions*. "He was called to Monterey on pressing duties, and the ceremonies were directed by Ensign Hermenegildo Sal, acting commandant at the Presidio of San Francisco, who arrived at Santa Cruz on September 22, 1791, accompanied by Fathers Isidro Alonzo Salazar and Baldomero Lopez of Mission Santa Clara, who were destined to be the first missionaries at the new station."

The fathers officially founded Mission Santa Cruz on September 25, 1791, in one of the most picturesque areas in California, 500 yards from the San Lorenzo River and across the Monterey Bay from Mission San Carlos Borromeo de Carmelo. The location was strategically a wise move for the Spanish Government, which wished to defend the area from foreign invasion by sea. The location also allowed easy access to ships bringing both food and supplies, as well as picking up goods for trade.

Additionally, the ocean provided a source of food if the crops were not sufficient to feed the Ohlone Indian neophytes. The flat land was conducive to farming and raising cattle, with the San Lorenzo River flowing close by to supply water for drinking and for irrigating the crops. Furthermore, wood from the redwood forests was easily accessible and abundant.

Missions Santa Clara, San Carlos, and Dolores contributed cows, oxen, steers, horses and mules to the new mission, and the buildings and church were erected in a short time. Unfortunately, flooding from the San Lorenzo River damaged the mission buildings, requiring a new church be built on higher ground.

It took more than a year to construct this church, which possessed five-foot-thick adobe walls supported by a three-foot-high stone foundation. Before long, the mission had established a flour mill, granary, and a building for looms. By 1795, the mission square was mostly completed.

The Ohlone Indians were hospitable and eager to share their foods with the Spanish explorers. And the Spanish padres introduced to the natives fruits such as watermelon and grapes, and vegetables including olives, beans, peppers, squash and corn. Grains of wheat, barley and oats, herbs, and nuts thrived in the mild coastal climate.

However, the mission took a turn for the worse when Villa Branciforte was founded on July 24, 1797, by Diego de Borica at the whim of Miguel de la Grúa Talamanca, Marqués de Branciforte, viceroy of Mexico, and against the pleas of Father Lasuén, President of the Missions. Villa Branciforte, one of Spain's few secular settlements in California, was intended to colonize the area, and the government encouraged settlers to move there. Unfortunately, in spite of the promise of a lucrative and thriving community, the settlers did not find the promised housing. Gambling and crime became prevalent, and with the threat of criminal activity so near, the Santa Cruz Mission did not experience the growth and success of other missions.

History notes the discordant relationship between the settlers and the mission. The fathers complained that the settlers were trespassing on the mission lands, but received no support or defense from the governor to protect the mission. With little to prohibit or punish their behavior, the settlers helped themselves to the agriculture produced by the neophytes and stole their livestock.

The fathers' restrictions on the Indians—intended to protect them from the influence of the Branciforte ruffians—caused increasingly hostile resentment. The padres at the mission kept a tight rein on their neophytes and prevented them from associating with the settlers. With such strict and cruel discipline, in 1812, a few of the Indians rebelled and murdered Father Andrés Quintana.

This incident contributed to the "bad luck" reputation the mission had earned. Although it appeared at first that the father had died in his sleep, some neophytes later confessed to his murder, stating their mistreatment as the reason for the attack. An autopsy was performed on the padre, the first one in California's medical history, to determine the cause of death, which was purported to be poisoning.

In 1818, when the pirate Hypolite Bouchard attacked Monterey, Governor Pablo Vicente de Solá ordered Father Ramon Olbés at Mission Santa Cruz to pack valuables and belongings and send them to Mission Soledad. The priest notified the townspeople of Branciforte to remove the property according to the governor's orders, and he and the mission Indians fled to Mission Santa Clara. The pirate did not invade Santa Cruz, and upon their return, Father Olbés discovered the mission had been ransacked not by the pirate but by the Branciforte general population.

By 1821, Mexico won independence from Spain, and the decline of the mission system was rapid. Mission Santa Cruz was the first mission to fall under the secularization

Original baptismal font

Mission Santa Cruz

decree from Mexico. In less than a year, most of the neophytes who were incapable of self-government had abandoned the mission, leaving too few to plant the crops and care for the dwindling livestock. An earthquake and tidal wave in 1840 demolished the bell tower, and another devastating earthquake on February 16, 1857, led to the complete destruction of the mission, which was already in disrepair due to neglect and vandalism.

Resurrected after California became a state in 1850, the Santa Cruz Mission and sixteen acres of surrounding land were returned to the Catholic Church by President James Buchanan in 1859. Another wooden church was constructed where the original adobe mission had been,

and then replaced again in 1889 by a large Gothic brick church, Church of the Holy Cross, which continues to serve the parishioners today.

Nothing remained, it was thought, of the mission complex, and in 1931 Mrs. Gladys Sullivan Doyle, inspired by the Mission Revival Movement, donated a replica one-half the size of the first mission, which was designed based on an oil painting of the original mission and from old records dating before its final collapse. This small facility across the street from the large brick church continues to serve the parishioners of the Church of the Holy Cross. In the small chapel and museum, relics from the previous era are sheltered in protective glass cases to allow viewing.

Original Indian residences

Among them are a chalice used by Father Serra, the mission's sandstone baptismal font, vestments, and other miscellaneous items used by the fathers.

Archeological digs and restoration have uncovered a large adobe section of the original mission complex about a half block from the mission replica. With secularization, the Indians were given the building, but in time they abandoned the remnants of the original mission structures. New settlers from Mexico became the next residents, and remodeled the building to accommodate their families.

The last remaining resident, Cornelia Hopcroft, at the age of 78, sold her home and the property to the State of California with the understanding she would live there until her death (she lived to the age of 104). It wasn't until after her death in 1983, when boards and sidings were stripped from the original adobe brick walls, that the Indian residence of the seven rooms remaining from the original seventeen was revealed. This building has since been restored as a museum and, according to a brochure called *Information about Santa Cruz Mission*, "This building is the only remaining example of Neophyte family housing for any of the California Missions."

Not far from the mission site is the Wilder Ranch State Park (originally the Rancho del Matadero), the main cattle ranch for the Santa Cruz Mission. The visitor center on the site illustrates the history shared between the ranch and the Mission, and offers visitors a glimpse into what Father Francisco Palóu envisioned.

Mission Santa Cruz is California State Landmark No. 342 and is on the National Register of Historic Places.

14 ∾ Mission Nuestra Señora de la Soledad

THE THIRTEENTH MISSION, Nuestra Señora de la Soledad, was dedicated to Most Holy Mary, "Our Lady of Solitude," which is a fitting name for this solitary place. It was the second mission to be named for Mary, mother of Jesus. The origins of the name "Soledad" are a mystery, but one theory is that Father Pedro Font—chaplain with Captain Juan B. Anza's expedition, credited with discovering the first overland route to San Francisco from Sonora, Mexico—noted in his diary that someone from General de Portolá's first expedition asked an Indian his name. The Indian answered "Soledad," which was then adopted as the name for the location.

Father Fermín Lasuén founded Mission Nuestra Señora de la Soledad on October 9, 1791, in a remote, desolate, wind-blown inland area overlooking a vast valley described as "bare brown plains" at the time. The mission was about thirty-five miles from Mission San Antonio, and was southwest of Mission San Carlos Borromeo de Carmelo.

Unlike the missions founded on the coast, Mission Soledad attracted few enthusiasts. The isolation deterred the trade that other missions thrived on, and goods and provisions were scarce. Twice, flooding from the Salinas and Arroyo Seco rivers destroyed the chapel and damaged other buildings. The cold and damp climate contributed to rheumatism, a common complaint from a number of priests, and the constant wind added to their discontent as well. Father Juan Crespí is reputed to have said that the Indians who came to Mission Soledad were "blown in by the four winds."

History also notes a departure of the exemplary long-suffering demeanor of the Franciscan padres. Two padres, Marino Rubi and Bartoleme Gili from the Missionary College of San Fernando de Mexico, were scoundrels, not worthy of the reputation of the Franciscans. Their previous antics at the college should have been grounds for dismissal, but instead they were assigned to Mission Soledad. Although they are credited with gaining converts while serving the mission for a year, their lack of patience with the Indians and their constant complaints about the hardship of life at the mission eventually resulted in their being recalled to Mexico.

Whereas most of the priests served just a short time at Mission Soledad before transferring to another mission, Father Florencio Ibañez devoted his life to the mission. Under his tutelage, the mission prospered for a period with livestock consisting of cattle and sheep, vineyards,

Mission Nuestra Señora de la Soledad

Landscape view west from Highway 101 looking toward the mission

and crops of wheat, corn, peas, and beans. The Salinas and Arroyo Seco rivers amply supplied water to the fields and the mission community. Unfortunately, in spite of the prosperity the mission briefly enjoyed, an epidemic in 1802 killed a number of natives, and the remaining Indians were frightened away, believing the new religion taught by the missionaries was the cause.

Rebounding, Mission Soledad's population increased over time to 688 neophytes by its heyday in 1805, but just five years later its population dwindled to the lowest number of converts amongst the missions, excepting that of Mission San Carlos.

The missions of California provided a place of respite and refuge for priests and any others who desired the quiet they afforded, and Mission Soledad was no exception.

Governor José Joaquín de Arrillaga, a good friend of Father Ibañez, fell severely ill on an inspection tour of the missions and was rushed to Mission Soledad, where he died on July 24, 1814. Arrillaga was the first Spanish governor of California and his term of office was called "The Golden Age of the Missions" because of his friendship with the Franciscans. He was buried beneath the chapel, as was Father Ibañez, when he died four years later. Ibañez is the only Franciscan to be buried at Mission Soledad.

Father Vicente Sarría, a one-time President of the California Missions, took on the role of serving as padre for the Soledad Mission because of his great love for the Indian wards of the mission. But the secularization decree of Governor Figueroa, who confiscated all the mission lands, proved to be an insurmountable obstacle. After Father Sarría died on May 24, 1835, and was buried at Mission San Antonio, the future of Mission Soledad was grim. By 1841, the mission was in ruins. No Indians or livestock were evident, and the vineyards and orchards were abandoned. On June 4, 1846, Governor Pío Pico sold the property to Feliciano Sobranes for $800.

The remnants of an adobe, red-tiled roof storeroom that has been converted into a chapel are virtually all that remain of the original mission complex, and there are few surviving records. The mission has no *companario*, but a single bell dating from the late 1700s that was cast in Mexico hangs from a wooden beam next to the chapel.

In November 1859, Mission Soledad was returned to the Catholic Church by President Buchanan.

Original adobe walls discovered in archeological digs

"Over the entrance of the church ... the ruins of which now bring sadness to the hearts of all who care ... is a niche in which a statue of Our Lady of solitude, La Soledad, used to stand. Methinks that if the ghosts of things that were exist, surely a weeping ghost of the Lady of Solitude haunts these deserted and forlorn ruins. Weep! Weep on! For the church of Our Lady of Solitude. It is entirely in ruins," said George Wharton James of Mission Soledad in 1904, while on a tour of the California missions (as noted by Kenneth C. Adams in *California Missions*.)

Ruins discovered by archeologists from the University of California, Los Angeles, illustrate the sun-baked adobe construction used in the quadrangle of the mission. In the cemetery behind the mission, the graves of both the first Spanish governor of California, Governor Arrillaga, and his close friend Father Ibañez, have been located exactly as historians recorded them years ago. Rising like a phoenix from the ashes, due to the restoration efforts of the Native Daughters of the Golden West begun in 1954, Mission Soledad is at last once again a mission worthy of attention.

Cross and bell on the north side of the mission wall

15 ∾ Mission San José de Guadalupe

By 1796, El Camino Reál linked Mission San Diego in southern Alta California to San Francisco's Mission Dolores in northern Alta California—two missions that were a considerable distance apart. Hostile bands of Indians threatened the settlers, missionaries, and other travelers on the El Camino Reál. The Presidio at San Francisco afforded some protection, but Father Fermín Lasuén thought it wise to request permission from the viceroy to establish five more missions along the route, intended to be within "a hard day's journey apart."

Mission San José de Guadalupe, founded by Father Lasuén on June 11, 1797, seems to have been established more for a military presence than to convert the peaceful Ohlone, Yokuts, Miwok, and Patwin Indians in the area.

Observing the dismal influence the Branciforte pueblo had on the Indians at Mission Santa Cruz, Father Lasuén chose a site that was fifteen miles north of the pueblo of San José to purposely separate the unruly colonists from the missionaries and neophytes.

But even with soldiers stationed both at the mission and at the San Francisco Presidio, tribes in the Sacramento and San Joaquin valleys of Central California and runaways from Mission Dolores continued to cause trouble. After a rather brutal attack on white travelers in 1805, the Spanish soldiers reacted, killing eleven Indians and capturing thirty more.

Mission San José de Guadalupe is located twelve miles from Mission Santa Clara, and it began with 600 head of cattle and a flock of seventy-eight sheep provided by Mission Santa Clara. The mission's population of neophytes grew slowly but steadily, from an original group of thirty-three to an eventual greater number of converts than any of the other missions before secularization.

Mission San José's buildings were constructed in the traditional mission quadrangle, spread out over five acres. The church was constructed of adobe and redwood hewn from the forests between Missions Santa Cruz and San José, and both its roof and floor were made of tile. The plain, whitewashed adobe walls were supported by buttresses, and the front entrance had semicircular brick steps.

The square bell tower attached to the church continues to hold one recast bell and three original bells, one of which weighs 1,000 pounds and in days past would ring out to announce the arrival of guests, the activities of the day, and to invite visitors to the mission.

In 1806, Father Narcisco Durán and Father Buenaventura Fortuny took over the helm of the San José Mission. Father Durán, using his natural musical talents, improvised musical instruments, and taught the Indians songs, chants, and hymns. After acquiring flutes, violins, trumpets, and drums from Mexico, he formed an Indian orchestra with thirty members and put on concerts and performed for weddings, fiestas, and feast days, drawing both pagans and Christians from the surrounding area to hear the musical entertainment.

Father Durán also devised an irrigation system to water the wheat and other crops, and he built aqueducts to direct warm water from the nearby hot springs for use in the *lavanderia* (outdoor laundry facility). Under his capable leadership, the mission grew to be the most successful of the northern missions and second only to Mission San Gabriel in the entire mission chain.

Raymund Wood writes in *A Brief History of Mission San José:* "Cattle had increased from 4,500 to 12,000 head, sheep from 8,000 to 13,000, and horses from 480 to 13,000. In 1832, the last harvest that Father Durán supervised, the yield was 6,400 bushels of wheat, 1,760 bushels of barley, and 1,700 bushels of corn, besides unspecified quantities of vegetables and fruits from the fields and orchards."

According to Wood, Father Durán's mission inventory, as listed in his final report, notes "…a church, monastery (priests' residence building), guardhouse, guest house, women's dormitory, winery, harness shop, shoe shop, candle shop, tailor shop, storeroom, granaries, weaving rooms, as well as homes for the Indians—enough of them to make a small town."

Father Durán served Mission San José for almost twenty-seven years, after which he served from 1837 to 1843 as Father-President of the California missions.

Among the notable historical figures who were welcome guests at the mission was Jedediah Smith, a trapper who braved the formidable Sierra Nevada, fighting not only nature but also hostile Indians. Smith found respite in both Mission San Gabriel and Mission San José in the years 1826 and 1827.

History notes an exceptional Indian rebellion in the story of Estanislao, a neophyte who had been born and raised at the mission. Elected chieftain, he was considered a favorite of Father Durán's. However, Estanislao decided

Wood cross on the side of the original padres' quarters

Mission San José de Guadalupe

to turn from mission life and rule over the rebellious tribes. The Indian community had been encouraged to periodically return to their people in order to strengthen the ties between the villages and the missionaries. During one of these visits, Estanislao did not return. He sent a letter to Father Durán stating his refusal to come back to the mission and claiming to have 500 people who would fight the soldiers, whom he considered to be just "mere boys." Father Durán enlisted the military to protect the mission, and a major battle ensued in the interior, with two expeditions mounted against the Indians ending in failure.

Mission cemetery

Estanislao, who was encouraged by his success in these campaigns, and sent a message to Father Durán proclaiming that he was now king of the Central Valley. A third military expedition was sent out and it too suffered defeat. The final revolt ended under the leadership of Lieutenant Mariano Vallejo (who was later promoted to general), who ordered the capture and execution of many Indians. Estanislao, aware of the impending outcome, fled to Mission San José and begged for forgiveness and sanctuary. Much as in the Biblical story of the Prodigal Son, Father Durán took him back. He then requested a pardon for Estanislao and his followers from Governor José Maria de Echeandía, which was granted on October 7, 1829.

Once the word was out that the formal pardon had been granted, many of the runaway neophytes returned to their missions. Estanislao lived peacefully at Mission San José until he came down with smallpox and died ten years later on July 31, 1838.

Kit Carson, another famous name in California's history, was in California in 1830 as a member of a trapping expedition under the command of Captain Ewing Young. While there, Carson fought on the side of the Mexicans to assist them in recapturing renegade runaways.

Captain Young was concerned that he did not have a license to trap in Mexico, and thought it wise to dispose of his pelts at Mission San José. A trade was made, and Captain Young and Kit Carson continued their trapping expedition, returning to the United States with horses and provisions provided by Father Durán.

After secularization in 1834, Mission San Joe, as it was known to the Gold Rush miners during the 1840s, became a thriving trading center for the exchange of gold.

Eventually, plundering and earthquakes took their toll, leaving just a remnant of the mission. In 1868, the Hayward Fault earthquake, California's strongest quake up to that time, destroyed the entire 5-acre quadrangle, except for the padres' west-wing living quarters. Later, a woodframe church and rectory were built over the remains of the original adobe mission foundation.

From 1982 to 1985, through restoration and preservation, a replica of the mission chapel was constructed, which included using floor tiles uncovered in archeological digs on the original site of the mission. Authentic artifacts in the museum illustrate the Ohlone Indians' craftsmanship and offer a history lesson on mission life at Mission San José de Guadalupe.

16 ∿ Mission San Juan Bautista

IRONICALLY, CONSIDERING the great damage earthquakes have done to the California missions, Mission San Juan Bautista—named in honor of Saint John the Baptist—was constructed directly over the San Andreas Fault. The mission was founded on June 24, 1797, by Father Fermín Lasuén on a site near Rio San Benito, on a mesa overlooking the San Juan Valley. Mission San Juan Bautista was the fifteenth California mission, and was the fourth mission to be founded in a brief three-month span.

Within six months, with the assistance of the friendly Mutsun Indians, a chapel, monastery, granary, guardhouse, barracks, and adobe housing for the neophytes had all been constructed. The padres, who were uncomfortable with the traditional marriage customs of the Indians they wished to civilize, had a building specifically set aside for unmarried Indian girls and women to dwell in until marriage.

A series of earthquakes between 1798 and 1803 demolished some of the buildings, yet they also offered an opportunity to rebuild and improve the mission church. With great pomp, on June 13, 1803, the cornerstone was laid for a much larger mission.

The San Juan Bautista mission church was the only one in the mission chain to feature a sanctuary with a central nave with two side aisles. It was also the largest of any of the Alta California mission churches: 72 by 188 feet, with walls three feet thick. The adobe construction was completed on June 25, 1812, after fifteen years of labor supplied by the padres and the Indians. Little more than six months later, the devastating earthquake of December 1812 shook the region. Fortunately, the mission's buildings, despite resting on the San Andreas Fault, were not damaged by the earthquake.

Mission San Juan Bautista was presented with a barrel organ made in England, believed to have been offered to the padres at Monterey by an English skipper. At first, the Indians were frightened by the noise, but they were so attracted to the sound of the music box that in time they overcame their fears and curiously gathered around the organ to listen. This musical introduction secured the Indians' loyalty to the mission.

Father Estévan Tápis later taught music to the mission youth. The singers he trained became so well

Mission San Juan Bautista

known that Mission San Juan Bautista was dubbed the "Mission of Music." Father Tápis designed sheet music on parchment that featured colored notes of red, yellow, black, and white, painted on the five music lines for the singers to follow. Today, Mission San Juan Bautista's museum displays these original parchment sheets.

Original Spanish plaza, the oldest in California

At the height of its prosperity, the mission owned 6,000 head of cattle, more than 6,000 sheep, twenty pigs, thirteen mules, and 296 horses.

In 1825, Governor José M. Echeandía set in motion the government actions that would eventually result in the end of the mission system. On January 1, 1826, Echeandía

Bell tower

issued a proclamation requiring all the missions to pay a "New Year's gift" of 10 percent of their income to the government to fund the military for their protection. This tax proved to be exorbitant to the missions, which, while self-sustaining, did not have the additional means to support the military.

By 1834, the Mexican government in Alta California, then under the rule of Governor José Figueroa, confiscated the missions with the intention of secularizing them. This proclamation, however, was not sanctioned by the Mexican government and was repudiated in 1835. Figueroa nevertheless proceeded with the confiscation process, and distributed the mission lands to Indian and Mexican ownership.

The Indians were declared "free," allowing them the ability to purchase the properties, but under the supervision of a paid majordomo with money and equipment to manage them. After the departure of the padres, the Indians abandoned the mission lands, and many returned to live with the nearby Tulare Indians.

"While at the end of 1836 the mission estate had still about 900 cattle and 4,000 sheep, with a crop of 900 bushels, and a debt of $1,300, there were no traces of a community. Constant depredations by savages, aided by ex-neophytes, from 1837 on contributed to the work of ruin," observed historian H. H. Bancroft, as recorded by Kenneth C. Adams in *California Missions*.

Throughout the mid- to late-1800s, padres continued to serve parishioners in the thriving Wild West town of San Juan Bautista. With the 1846 raising of the American flag over Monterey, the United States military was ordered to protect the missions. On November 19, 1859, President James Buchanan decreed Mission San Juan Bautista be returned to the Catholic Church.

The 1906 earthquake destroyed many of the mission's buildings, including the church. Also destroyed was an orphanage managed by the Sisters of the Immaculate Heart of Mary, who had come from Spain specifically to establish a day school and orphanage at the mission.

With funding from the William Randolph Hearst Foundation in 1949, as well as by various funds raised through fiestas and commemorative days, Mission San Juan Bautista has been restored and now surpasses the stature it had in 1812. During reconstruction, the stucco bell tower was removed and the bells were temporarily hung on a wooden crossbar in front of the mission. A reconstructed Spanish-style *campanario*, much like the design used for Mission San Diego, now houses the three bells, two of which remain from the mission's original nine bells. An arched colonnade has been restored from the existing arches of the mission church, and the floor of the church still possesses its original tiles.

The plaza facing the mission is the last surviving Spanish plaza in California, and has been designated a State Historical Monument. The guard unit of soldiers assigned to the mission lived in barracks located beneath the site of the present-day Plaza Hotel. Rangers with the California Parks and Recreation Department have set up quarters in the Plaza Hotel to care for the San Juan Bautista State Historic Park.

In 1996, the Guadalupe chapel was restored. Planned future restoration projects, under the auspices of Dr. Ruben Mendoza and students at California State University, Monterey Bay, include rebuilding the guard tower and restoring the missing wings of the mission foundations.

The town of San Juan Bautista is rich in early California history, and the mission continues to serve a largely Spanish-speaking parish. The town and mission are surrounded by lush farmland, ranches with herds of livestock, and orchards with pears and apples growing in abundance. Adjacent to the remains of the old stone wall beneath the cemetery, a short length of the original El Camino Reál footpath stretches from the flat agricultural fields to the central plaza in front of Mission San Juan Bautista.

17 ～ Mission San Miguel Arcángel

WHEN VICEROY BRANCIFORTE in Mexico approved the sixteenth mission on El Camino Reál, Father-President of the Missions Fermín Lasuén proceeded to found Mission San Miguel Arcángel in honor of "The most glorious Prince of the Celestial Militia, Archangel St. Michael." Father Lasuén blessed the site and raised the cross on July 25, 1797, on a spot near the Salinas River known by the Indians as Cholam. The Spaniards referred to it as "Paraza de Las Pozas."

Midway between Mission San Antonio de Padua and Mission San Luis Obispo de Tolosa, Mission San Miguel Arcángel was located near the hot springs in Paso Robles, revered by the Indians for their medicinal value.

The Indians in the area, familiar with the work of other missions, welcomed the newcomers and willingly began the work of building the mission under the guidance of Father Buenaventura Sitjar and Father Antonio de la Concepcíon Horra (who was soon removed because of insanity).

A permanent structure of stone foundations with approximately six-foot-wide adobe walls was constructed to replace the initial temporary wooden church, and by 1806 adobe huts had been constructed for the neophytes. However, a devastating earthquake destroyed the church and other mission buildings that same year.

A new stone church was constructed from 1816 to 1818, with large wooden beams transported to the mission from forty miles away. The church is simple in design on the exterior, but boasts one of the most elaborate interiors of any of the missions.

Spanish artist Estévan Munras of Monterey, a close friend of Father Juan Cabot, supervised the Indians' work in creating vibrant frescoes and murals of blue, green, pink, and brown on the mission's walls and ceiling. Much of this artwork still remains.

The size and order of the arches in the front of the padres' living quarters are unusual in that the mission has twelve arches, similar to other missions, but not of equal size or shape. They are arranged symmetrically: small and semicircular at the ends of the row; four large arches in the center, with a large, elliptical arch on either side of the center arch.

The 200-foot-square quadrangle consisted of workshops for leather, carpentry, weaving, stonework, and ironwork, in which the Indians honed their craftsmanship.

Sophisticated water systems involving a gristmill, reservoirs, and aqueducts moved water from the Salinas

Mission San Miguel Arcángel

River to the mission and fields. Mission San Miguel's vast land holdings extended eighteen miles to the north, eighteen miles to the south, sixty miles east, and thirty-five miles west to the Pacific Ocean. It would have been impossible for the mission padres to oversee such an expansive operation, but the well-trained Indian converts managed the tasks within their own communities, tending

Campanile, separate from the mission

vineyards and crops of wheat and barley. The mission averaged 22,000 head of livestock as well, which grazed on mission ranchos from 1811 to 1824.

With Mission San Miguel Arcángel prosperous and experiencing little in the way of conflicts, the fathers put aside their longstanding priority of founding coastal missions and looked to the expansive Central Valley for their next mission site.

Several expeditions were sent out, but the hostile Tulare Indians resented the white man's intrusion, whether by settler or missionary. Given this situation, coupled with the growing antagonism of the Mexican civil authorities, the plan was abandoned.

Governor José Echeandía issued a decree on January 6, 1831, to immediately begin the secularization of the California missions. Commissioner Juan B. Alvarado gathered the neophytes together at Mission San Miguel Arcángel and attempted to assure them that their trials were over. According to a 1922 article titled "Secularization of the Missions":

> No tyrannical priest could compel them to work. They were to be citizens in a free and glorious republic, with none to molest or make them afraid. Then he called for those who wished to enjoy these blessings of freedom 'to come to the right,' while those who were content to remain under the hideous bondage of the missions could go to the left. Imagine his surprise and the chill his oratory received when all but a small handful quickly went to the left, and those who at first went to the right speedily joined the majority.

San Miguel was one of the last missions to be secularized, and its last remaining Franciscan, Father Abella, left in

July 1841. Governor Pío Pico sold Mission San Miguel on July 4, 1846, to Petronillo Rios and William Reed, who used the mission as a residence for their families.

Reed enjoyed bragging to visitors about the gold he had accumulated, and it was assumed the gold was hidden somewhere at the former mission. Five men, after hearing of the wealth that could be theirs, left after their visit to the mission, but later returned, killed Reed, his child, and his wife and her family, and took his gold and other valuables. A citizen posse took chase and killed one man, another drowned in the sea, and the remaining three were captured.

In the book *The Missions and Missionaries of California, San Miguel Arcángel.*, Father Engelhardt reported:

> What action was taken is best related in the words of Governor Mason. Reporting to the Adjutant General of the U.S. Army at Washington under date of January 17, 1849, among other information on California, the Governor writes as follows: "I regret to report that several most horrible murders have of late been committed in this country. The entire occupants of the Mission of San Miguel—men, women, and children—in all ten [eleven] persons, were murdered about two weeks ago, and there is no doubt that the murders were committed by white men.... Upon hearing of the murder of Mr. Reed's family at Mission San Miguel, I dispatched Lieutenant Ord with a couple of men to that Mission to ascertain the truth, and, if need, to aid the *alcalde* in the execution of his office.

Front arcade view with fountain

Cross carved into tree bark to mark the El Camino Reál trail

As it was reported that five men had been found, with strong evidence of guilt, I told Lieutenant Ord to inform the *alcalde* that if the evidence were clear and positive, and the sentence of the jury were death, he might cause it to be executed without referring the case to me. This course is absolutely necessary, as there are no jails or prisons in the country, where a criminal can be safely secured." The three merciless brutes were accordingly executed at Santa Bárbara on December 28, 1848.

The coming of the Gold Rush to California brought gamblers, and the convenience of Mission San Miguel's location on El Camino Reál made the "Mission on the Highway" a convenient refuge. Part of the mission became a saloon and dance hall. A sewing machine company used another building. However, the ruffians in the area seemed to believe the church was sacred, so it was not damaged.

President James Buchanan returned San Miguel Mission to the Catholic Church on September 2, 1859, but it wasn't until 1878 that Bishop Francis Mora appointed the Reverend Philip Farrely to pastor the church. Farrely and his successors diligently began work to restore the mission.

Museums are now housed in former priests' living quarters, illustrating the customs of life in a monastery during the mission era. An exhibit shows hides of sheep and cattle that were used for makeshift windows until glass could be installed. The hides were stretched over a wooden frame, then shaved and greased to create transparent "windows." Other exhibits include spinning wheels and looms, the traditional beehive oven, and ironworks.

A large tree trunk displays a cross, which has been carved into its side. The notation for this exhibit explains that the padres used the symbol of the carved cross to guide travelers on El Camino Reál.

A devastating earthquake on December 22, 2003, did considerable damage to the church, but extensive restoration is bringing back the glory that was Mission San Miguel. The Mission San Miguel sanctuary reopened in the fall of 2009 and the murals, considered to be some of the finest examples of Spanish art in America, again inspire viewers. In addition, a large six foot bronze statue of Jesus standing erect with arms outstretched, sculpted by Dorothy Boyle and cast by the Genesis Bronze foundry from Paso Robles, is expected to be unveiled by Easter 2010.

Mission San Miguel is on the National Register of Historic Places and was designated a National Historic Landmark by the National Park Service, U.S. Department of the Interior.

18 ∾ Mission San Fernando Rey de España

THE "MISSION OF THE VALLEY" is located in an area discovered by Father Juan Crespí in 1769, while he was a member of Gaspár de Portolá's expedition. Impressed by the fertile land, well-suited for agriculture, and the four streams flowing nearby, Crespí recommended the site to Father Serra for the Franciscan mission chain. Years later, on September 8, 1797, Father Fermín Lasuén founded Mission San Fernando Rey de España, dedicated in honor of the king of Spain.

Mission San Fernando Rey de España is located on El Camino Reál, overlooking El Valle de Santa Catalina de Bononia de los Encinos, between Missions San Gabriel and San Buenaventura. The seventeenth California mission, San Fernando Rey de España would be the fourth mission founded in the three-month period from June to September 1797.

The first mission church was a small adobe building, where forty-three baptisms took place on the day of its dedication. All baptisms prior to these had been performed in the little arbor where the mission's first Holy Mass was held. Rapid growth brought about the construction of granaries and quarters for the Indians, priests, and soldiers. A second church was built by 1799, followed by the construction of a much larger church by 1806.

Mission San Fernando enjoyed prosperity until the Mexican revolt against Spain in 1810. From then on, the mission supported the soldiers and their families with provisions of food, clothing, and money.

Mission San Fernando was subject to earthquake damage, and damage from the earthquake of 1812 required extensive repairs and reinforcement to the church walls. The rebuilt mission completed in 1822 was picturesque, with its long, arched *convento* corridor known as the "House of the Fathers." The unusual corridor, featuring twenty-one Roman arches, runs the length of the entire mission, although it is separate from the church. The church is situated in the back of the mission quadrangle.

Not only was the colonnade unusual, but the two-story *convento* is noted for being the largest adobe building in California at 243 feet long and 50 feet wide. A large library is maintained in these quarters and is considered to house one of the oldest collections in California, after those at Missions Carmel and Santa Bárbara.

Although Governor Echeandía, who governed from 1825 to 1830, planned a takeover of Mission San Fernando to create a pueblo, free the Indians, and assign a missionary to pastor the Indians, he failed to accomplish this plan.

Governor Manuel Victoria, who succeeded Echeandía in 1830, sought to help the Franciscan missions, but his reign was short-lived due to the overthrow of his government by Pío Pico (whose followers included Echeandía). Pico governed for two months, from January to February in 1832. Then Augustín V. Zamorano—a statesman, craftsman, and California's first printer—and Echeandía divided California into two areas, with Zamorano governing to the north of San Fernando and Echeandía governing to the south. Finally, José Figueroa came into power in 1833, and on August 9, 1834, he decreed the seizure of all mission lands.

In an interesting aside, legend has it that the first discovery of gold in California, on March 8, 1842, was located near Mission San Fernando. According to *California Missions: A Guide to the State's Spanish Heritage,* Majordomo Francisco Lopez "found shiny yellow particles clinging to some roots from a bunch of onions. From then

The 21 arches of the corridor are separate from the church in the back

Mission San Fernando Rey de España

until the discovery of gold at Sutter's Mill in northern California, the Placerita Canyon area northwest of San Fernando became the focus of intense prospecting." The guide also describes a rumor that the missionaries of San Fernando found and hoarded the gold. Because of this rumor, vandals later dug through the mission grounds searching for the "dead monks' treasure."

By 1845, Pío Pico was again governor, and he leased the mission lands to his brother, Andres. Virtually abandoned in 1847 after America seized California from Mexico, Mission San Fernando was used for various purposes: a stagecoach station, a warehouse, and a stable, as well as quarters for Colonel John C. Frémont and his army. Finally, on May 31, 1862, President Lincoln restored Mission San Fernando Rey de España back to the Catholic Church.

Restoration, begun in 1916 under the preservation efforts of the Landmarks Club, has recreated the former beauty of the mission. The large original star-shaped fountain of Moorish design, patterned after one in Cordova, Spain, and built by Indians under the guidance of the fathers more than a hundred years ago, still exists.

The fountain, along with two stone vats, was moved from the front of the mission to Brand Park, directly across the street. In 1920, the Mission Land Company deeded Brand Park to the City of Los Angeles. Brand Park features a "Memory Garden" with olive trees dedicated to those who contributed to the American conquest of California, as well as pepper trees grown from seeds taken from the first pepper tree in California, which was located at Mission San Luis Rey de Francia. Other rare trees and cacti fill the gardens with colorful seasonal flowers and roses.

Unfortunately, an earthquake in 1971 caused so much damage to the original structure that Mission San Fernando had to be completely rebuilt. On November 4, 1974, Cardinal Timothy Manning dedicated the replica and the restored *convento*.

Hollywood has discovered the mission's beauty and frequently uses the mission and grounds for filming. Many community events take place there as well. A beautiful private garden and gravesite monument to entertainer Bob Hope is located in the San Fernando Mission cemetery. It was said that in making long-range plans for burial, his wife asked Bob where he wanted to be buried. He said, "Surprise me," so she did by having him buried on the grounds of the mission he loved so well. Bob Hope died on July 27, 2003.

Original fountain of Moorish design in Brand Park across from the mission

19 ∾ Mission San Luis Rey de Francia

FATHER FERMÍN LASUÉN founded his ninth and last mission on a hill overlooking a coastal valley, pleased with its crucial location between San Diego and Mission San Juan Capistrano. Mission San Luis Rey de Francia, named in honor of Louis IX, king of France, is familiarly known as "The King of the Missions." Founded on June 13, 1789, Mission San Luis Rey is the eighteenth of the California missions.

Being gifted with a talent for both architecture and management, Father Antonio Peyri was appointed by Father Lasuén to administer the mission and to supervise the labor provided by the Indians and soldiers from the San Diego Presidio to build the mission. Within the first year, Indian accommodations and a temporary church had been constructed.

A new church, able to accommodate a congregation of 1,000 people, was built from 1811 to 1815. It featured adobe bricks set in a diagonal pattern, and spanned a length of 165 feet, a width of 27 feet, and a height of 30 feet. The cruciform design of the church was similar to that of only one other mission in the chain, the Great Stone Church of San Juan Capistrano. The long, narrow length was crossed by a section holding two side altars, with a tall tower at the crossing. The top of the tower had an octagonal lantern with a design of eight columns and 144 panes of glass, the only mission with this feature.

This octagonal lantern eventually would be replaced with a round dome, an element unique to this mission.

Under Father Peyri's guidance, the mission grounds expanded to six acres, and enjoyed an elaborate water system derived from a nearby river. Directly across from the mission, a small valley boasted a lush sunken garden containing rare and exotic plants and trees. A brick wall enclosed the garden, with stone steps leading to the ground level where the ruin of the mission's *lavanderia* are still evident.

Mission San Luis Rey grew rapidly and soon had a population of more than 1,500 neophytes. To manage the growth and meet the needs of those Indians somewhat distant from the mission, Father Peyri established the San Antonio de Pala Asistencia on June 13, 1816.

The *asistencia* was built on the Pala rancheria, close to Mount Palomar, and about twenty miles inland from the mission. Interestingly, the Pala rancheria was the location initially recommended for the mission site; however, it was decided that the spot was not feasible, being too far removed from El Camino Reál.

The San Antonio de Pala sub-mission became so successful that it rivaled the wealth of its mentor mission. A chapel, granary, and other buildings were built, and the fertile valley produced bountiful grain crops. It had long been the dream of Father Serra to establish a chain of inland missions, and the Pala sub-mission served that vision well.

Although Mission San Luis Rey de Francia prospered, it did so while confronting challenges. On numerous occasions, Father Peyri complained about the soldiers encroaching on mission lands. In time, an enmity developed between the military and the priests, even though Father Peyri had signed a loyalty oath to Mexico.

Perhaps disillusioned by the heavy demands of the territorial government, Father Peyri requested a reassignment back to Spain. He tried to slip away without notice, but 500 neophytes came after him, finally reaching him at San Diego as his ship was leaving. They begged him to stay, but he gently refused, blessed them, and left.

Father Peyri, credited for the mission's extraordinary population of Indian converts, as well as its wealth, served the mission for thirty-four years, from 1798 to 1832.

In 1834, the government of Mexico seized Mission San Luis Rey's lands, buildings, property, sacred vessels, and vestments, as well as the six ranchos owned and operated by the padres and their Indian converts. These various assets were valued at "$203,737.37 and outstanding debts were listed at $9,300.87," writes Kenneth C. Adams in *California Missions*.

Gate to the sunken garden

Mission San Luis Rey de Francia

Prior to Father Peyri's departure, 2,819 Indians lived at the mission, and livestock consisted of 26,000 head of cattle, 25,500 sheep, 1,200 goats, 2,150 horses, 250 mules, and 300 pigs, notes Adams.

The secularization act devastated Mission San Luis Rey. Those padres and Indians who remained at the mission became tenants. Many of the Indians fled the mission and returned to their former ways; others were enslaved under the brutal administration of the mission's new owners, Captain Portilla and former governor Pío Pico, who became mission administrator.

Prospects for Mission San Luis Rey brightened with the appointment of William Hartnell as inspector of the missions. Pío Pico was removed from his position. José Antonio Estudillo of San Diego followed, but Pico continued to seize the mission's ranchos. Under the leadership of Governor Manuel Micheltorena in 1843, the San Luis Rey mission was returned to the Franciscans; however, the ensuing peace ended with the return of Pico as governor. Resolved to put an end to the California mission system, on May 18, 1846, Pico sold the mission, as well as the sub-mission, San Antonio de Pala, to José A. Cot and José A. Pico for $2,000 in silver and $437.50 worth of grain.

The sale was declared illegal when the United States took possession of California, which allowed Mission San Luis Rey to start its long process of rebuilding. On March 18, 1861, some of the California missions were returned to the Catholic Church by President Abraham Lincoln's decree.

The "King of the Missions," Mission San Luis Rey de Francia, was designated a Franciscan seminary in 1893, and seminarians began extensive restoration on the quadrangle and the mission church. Today, the quadrangle has been restored, revealing a single original arch standing at the entrance to an enclosed garden. Rare specimens of plants in the garden include the first pepper tree in California, a tree species which became a staple

Original mission arch leading to garden

First pepper tree in California

San Antonio de Pala Asistencia *campanario,* separate from the mission

in California mission gardens, as the peppercorns were dried and ground to season the meals prepared for the mission community.

San Antonio de Pala Asistencia

Secularization also took its toll on San Antonio de Pala Asistencia, which saw its crops, livestock, and property confiscated. Perhaps because of its remote inland location on the Pauma Indian Reservation, the original buildings remain well preserved. The *asistencia* was returned to the Catholic Church in 1903 and possesses the only chapel in the mission chain to continuously serve the Indians as a parish church.

Father Peyri provided the design for the San Antonio de Pala Asistencia. The campanile of the *asistencia,* architecturally distinctive for its separation from the mission church and quadrangle, offers an elegant addition, rising fifty feet upward and containing two bell niches. The bells date from restoration work done in 1916 and are engraved with Biblical inscriptions.

An unusual detail on the campanile is a cactus growing on the roof of the tower. Legend has it that Father Peyri, pleased with his completion of the *asistencia,* crowned the tower with the "Christian symbol of victory." Atop the tower is a cross, and beneath the cross is displayed the cactus, which symbolizes victory over the wilderness.

20 ～ Mission Santa Inés

MISSION SANTA INÉS is known as the "Hidden Gem of the Missions" and the "Mission of the Passes" for its location in the Santa Ynez Valley, between the Santa Inés and San Rafael mountains. Built on what was once a rancheria named after Alajulapua, a Chumash villager, Mission Santa Inés is the nineteenth mission in the mission chain and the fourth to honor a woman, Saint Agnes.

Father Estévan Tápis, who succeeded Father Fermín Lasuén as the superior, raised the cross and blessed the Mission Santa Inés site on September 17, 1804.

The mission site was ideal for establishing a military presence between missions La Purísima Concepcíon and Santa Bárbara, and the fertile land offered the potential for growth. However, the local Indians, who were friendly with the warring Tulare Indian tribes from the Sierra, threatened the mission. Nevertheless, Father Tápis began his ministry by baptizing a number of children, before taking his departure and leaving Fathers José Antonio Calzada and Romualdo Gutierrez in charge.

Between 1804 and 1812, the mission church, living quarters for the fathers and soldiers, and homes for 400 neophytes were built. Granaries and a warehouse brought the total of new construction to more than eighty adobe buildings. The Chumash Indians' craftsmanship with leather and metal was unparalleled, especially in their silver-decorated saddles, candlesticks, and other items made from metal and copper. Father Francisco Javier de

Uría, who replaced Fathers Calzada and Gutierrez during the 1808 to 1824 period, designed a sophisticated water system with underground clay pipes that transported the water from the mountains to two reservoirs.

Although Mission Santa Inés grew rapidly and became well known for large herds of cattle and abundant crops of wheat and corn, the Mexican revolt against Spain in 1810 burdened this mission with demands from Mexico to supply the military at the Santa Bárbara Presidio with clothing and provisions.

The earthquake of December 21, 1812, demolished buildings and destroyed the church. But Father Uría was undaunted, and he designed a new church, which was dedicated five years later.

The classic mission architectural style of Mission Santa Inés was similar to that of Mission San Gabriel. The sanctuary and long corridor, housing twenty-two arches, were constructed of five-foot-thick adobe and brick supports, and were further supported by buttresses to enable them to withstand the destruction of earthquakes.

Valley landscape between Santa Lucia and the Santa Inés mountains

The entrance to the church featured two carved wooden doors, with an arched window above. The tile roof was supported by beams and rafters hewn from oak, sycamore, and pine, held together with strips of rawhide. Large, square, brick tiles covered the floor, similar in design to Mission San Fernando Rey de España.

On February 21, 1824, Indians, who resented providing their labor to support the military, staged a massive rebellion, which included attacks against the Santa Bárbara and Purísima Concepción missions. Although the Indians burned the workshops and the soldiers' and guards' quarters at Mission Santa Inés, they had a change of heart when the church was threatened, and instead fought to save it.

Mission Santa Inés continued to prosper for many years, despite experiencing turmoil and unrest, stemming not just from the Indians, but also from the constantly changing and oppressive administrations governing California. But by 1836, Santa Inés faced demise under secularization. Assets of the mission and property at this time were estimated to be $56,437.62, with debts of $5,475.

In May 1839, mission inspector William Hartnell found the mission to be in a desperate condition. More changes came when Manuel Micheltorena from Mexico came to California and was installed on December 31, 1842, as the new governor. He was instructed by official decree from the Mexican government to return the missions to the Franciscans.

In *California Missions*, Kenneth C. Adams notes: "And on March 16, 1844, Micheltorena, at the request of Father Jimeno and Juan Moreno of Santa Inés and Father Francisco Sanchez of the seminary at Santa Bárbara, deeded to the padres land on which to erect a seminary college, granted them $500.00 a year for school maintenance, and later gave additional land which placed a total of 35,499 acres under control of the college."

The first college seminary in California, College of Our Lady of Refuge of Sinners, founded in 1844, by the first bishop of California, Francisco Garcia Diega y Moreno, lasted two years before new Governor Pío Pico and his followers

Ruins of original arch #19

banished Micheltorena from California and confiscated the mission property in 1846. However, since the 35,500 acres had been a gift to the padres from the previous Governor Micheltorena, Pico was not able to seize that land. The college was transferred to the Picpus Fathers of South America in 1850, then to the Christian Brothers in

1877, and later finally closed. The college was eventually sold to private ownership.

Three weeks after Mission Santa Inés was sold, Pico fled to Baja California as the American flag was raised in Monterey.

On May 23, 1862, the California missions were returned to the Catholic Church. For several years the care and management of the College of Our Lady of Refuge of Sinners—the first seminary and institution of higher learning in California—went from the governance of the Franciscans to other orders, before returning to the Franciscans. Finally, the school was closed, and the 35,500-acre property used for the college was sold.

In July 1904, Father Alexander Buckler was appointed to Mission Santa Inés by Bishop Thomas James Conaty, D. D., of Los Angeles, to begin restoration of the mission. He devoted the rest of his life to restoring the mission with the aid of his niece, Miss Mary [Mamie] Goulet. According to Kenneth Adams, assistance was also provided by the "'Dick Turpins,' as they called them. They were the tramps, hobos and wayfarers who happened by the mission over a period of years and were fed, housed, and put to work on the mission by the padre."

In 1911, rainstorms caused the bell tower to collapse and slowed the restoration effort, but again, Bishop Conaty, with the aid of the Knights of Columbus of Los Angeles, provided the funds to continue the restoration. In 1947, another grant was provided by the William Randolph Hearst Foundation.

Restoration efforts have revealed the mission's twenty-two arches. Whereas eighteen of the original arches have been fully restored, number nineteen reflects the ruins of the original arch as a reminder of the destruction and neglect of the mission under secularization.

Four bells, one dated 1818 and recast in 1953, another dated 1912, and two recent bells dedicated in 1984, hang in niches in the *campanario* at the side of the church. Bells were an integral part of mission life; they were rung to announce prayer, to toll for the deceased, to celebrate marriages, to signal the announcement of a padre, or to warn of danger.

Additional mission bells dating from 1804, 1807, and 1817 are displayed in the historical museum. Collections of handmade parchment music, Latin missals, and original paintings, as well as garments repaired and preserved by Mamie Goulet, are also on display.

Today, Mission Santa Inés continues to be an active parish under the governance of the Capuchin Franciscan Order of the Irish Province. Designs symbolizing the "River of Life" are carved into the old wooden doors of Mission Santa Inés, and the stately old mission continues to overlook fields seemingly untouched in 200 years.

Mission Santa Inés

21 ∾ Mission San Rafael Arcángel

FATHER VICENTE SARRÍA founded Mission San Rafael Arcángel, dedicated to the Archangel Saint Raphael, on December 14, 1817. The mission, located just fifteen miles north of San Francisco, was originally intended to be an *asistencia* for Mission San Francisco de Asís. San Rafael Arcángel was designed specifically for the care and hospitalization of the neophytes who had taken ill with white men's diseases. More than 200 patients came from Mission Dolores in San Francisco, and as the word spread to the rest of the missions, other neophytes benefited from the hospital as well. Father Luis Gil y Taboada was chosen to administer the church because he was the most familiar with medical science.

This *asistencia*, or sub-mission, was intended to be primarily a sanitarium. However, its establishment also furthered a strategic goal to establish missions and a presidio even farther north than San Francisco. The construction of Mission San Rafael helped to thwart the Russians, who were well-established at Fort Ross in the Bodega Bay area.

Mission San Rafael Arcángel did not possess the size or stature of the other California missions. It was small, encompassing just a chapel, baptistry, and cemetery. By 1818, the church, priests' housing, and hospital apartments were added. The Indians had no accommodations and lived in small huts surrounding the few buildings. The size of the mission complex was 87 feet long, 42 feet wide, and 18 feet high, with tules making up the roof. The church had no bell tower, so the mission bells hung outside the small chapel on a wooden frame. The mission's layout did not resemble traditional mission design, as it lacked a quadrangle.

Bells to the left of the church entrance

Mission San Rafael Arcángel

However, under Father Juan Amorós, who succeeded Father Gil y Taboada in 1819, the *asistencia* thrived to such an extent that the small hospital outpost was granted full mission status in 1822. Mission San Rafael Arcángel was self-sufficient, self-supporting, and prosperous enough to send supplies and goods to the presidio in San Francisco.

Father Amorós served the mission for thirteen years until his death on July 14, 1832, at which time Father Jesus Maria y José Guadalupe de la Trinidad Vasquez del Mercado supervised the mission for the remaining two years prior to secularization. His volatile temper and personality aggravated conflicts with mission Indians and

Replica of Mission San Rafael Arcángel, with present parish church built in 1917

with General Mariano Vallejo, the military commandant of California. General Vallejo subsequently moved the Indians to his own lands to work for room and board, acquired much of the mission assets, and transferred the mission livestock to his ranches.

Mission San Rafael Arcángel was the first mission to be seized after secularization. It was sold to Antonio M. Pico and his associates for 8,000 pesos on October 28, 1844, but the title was later declared void after the United States took possession of California. Even though the Indians received the mission properties, they proved unable to manage them.

By 1846, the mission was deserted and the buildings were crumbling. Captain John C. Frémont took possession of the property in June of that year to use for military quarters during the United States' battle with Mexico for possession of California. In 1855, after the United States' successful seizure of California, the mission and its six-and-a-half acres were returned to the Diocese of San Francisco. However, the buildings were in ruins, and the mission was sold to James Byers, a carpenter, in 1861. The Catholic parishioners moved to Saint Vincent Orphanage for services, and in the 1860s, gypsies camped on the former mission grounds.

In 1869, the Catholic Church built a parish church on the site of the original mission. When this church burned down on January 11, 1919, a new one was built. It remains at A Street in San Rafael, next to an adjoining parochial school.

"All that finally remained of the hospital mission was a single pear tree from the old mission orchard, until the restoration of the chapel in 1949. Monsignor Thomas

A pear branch, symbolic of the single pear tree located in the orchard remaining from the original mission era

Kennedy, the present pastor of San Rafael Church, says he recently transplanted a small tendril from that ancient tree, hoping to keep some part of it as a living symbol of the spirit of Father Amorós and the old Mission San Rafael Arcángel. Of course the tiny tree will live," wrote author Mary Null Boule in her book *Mission San Rafael Arcángel*.

As no drawings or photographs of the original mission remained in existence, an approximate replica of what the original church might have resembled, with a simple door under a star window, was financed by a grant provided by the William Randolph Hearst Foundation. Bells similar to those that might have been used originally hang on a wooden frame outside the church, just to the left of the entrance.

22 ~ Mission San Francisco Solano de Sonoma

AFTER FIFTY-FOUR YEARS, Father Serra's vision of establishing Franciscan missions the length of Alta California on or near El Camino Reál, "The Trail of the Padres," finally came to an end with the founding of Mission San Francisco Solano de Sonoma.

Mission San Francisco Solano de Sonoma was founded by Father José Altimira on July 4, 1823, in the Valley of the Moon, the last Franciscan mission of the twenty-one California missions. The name was chosen in honor of Saint Francis Solano, a Peruvian missionary.

Mission Sonoma, as it was familiarly known, was established as a result of various political tensions unique to its situation. It was the only mission founded under Mexican rule and without the authorization of the President of the California Missions.

Father President Vicente Sarría protested the new mission's founding. "The first important matter which engaged the attention of Father Sarría was the unauthorized founding of a new mission in the north and the attempted suppression of the missions of San Francisco and San Rafael," wrote mission historian Father Zephyrin Engelhardt in *The Missions and Missionaries of California*.

Father Altimira's desire to establish Mission Sonoma as the northernmost mission succeeded, in part due to a compromise reached between Father Sarría and Governor

Don Luis Argüello. The governor, who insisted that the Franciscans had not made enough neophyte conversions in the north, wanted to put the mission under governmental control. To avoid having a mission ruled under secular authority, Father Sarría allowed Mission Sonoma to be built, and governed under Father Altimira, but he refused to close Missions San Francisco and San Rafael.

Initial construction consisted of a small wooden church, granaries, and quarters for the missionaries. Although thwarting the Russian expansionist threat at Fort Ross to the north was a key factor in establishing Mission San Francisco Solano, the Russians generously sent contributions of linens, utensils, and bells to the fledgling outpost, and soon trade opened between the Russian fort and the mission.

Orchards and vineyards (including the first vineyard in Sonoma Valley) located on the 10,000 acres of mission land, thrived in the ideal climate of northern California. With substantial contributions of Indians from Missions San José, Dolores, and San Rafael, by the end of 1824, the neophyte population totaled 693. The first baptisms took

Mission San Francisco Solano de Sonoma

place in the small wooden chapel, and soon a granary and the padres' quarters were completed.

Father Altimira, unlike most of the Franciscan missionaries, believed in harsh punishments of flogging and imprisonment for his disobedient neophytes. Consequently, with no presidio or guard to protect the mission, the Indians revolted and vandalized the mission in 1826. Father Altimira fled to San Rafael and then moved on to Europe.

Father Buenaventura Fortuny succeeded him and, given his kinder disposition, was able to win the Indians' trust. The Indians provided the labor to build adobe residences for the 1,000 neophytes and completed the quadrangle within ten years. Later, Father Fortuny laid

Mission corridor, with a view of General Vallejo's barracks as they appear today

the foundation for a much larger adobe church east of the original padres' quarters.

But the mission was established too late to become as prosperous as many of the other missions. In 1834, Mexico seized control and established General Mariano Vallejo as commissioner. Under secularization, mission properties were distributed to the Indians, but with settlers and other hostile Indians persecuting the neophytes, General Vallejo offered the mission Indians room, board, and protection in exchange for their work. Vallejo proceeded with Mexico's order to establish a pueblo surrounding the mission and to erect homes for the Mexican colonists. Soldiers were transferred from the San Francisco Presidio to Sonoma to maintain Mexico's holdings against a possible Russian invasion or any other threat from the north.

With no active mission community, the buildings crumbled, and settlers and ranchers confiscated everything of value. In 1841, General Vallejo constructed and furnished a small adobe parish church to replace the old mission church on the original site of Father Altimira's wooden chapel. In 1845, Governor Pío Pico offered the mission ruins for sale, although there were no takers.

A growing unrest smoldered among the American settlers, who decided to form a republic independent from Mexican control. Working with Captain John Charles Frémont, these settlers captured General Vallejo and took control of Sonoma. A crude flag featuring a grizzly bear and the words "California Republic" was raised on June 14, 1846. Attempts were made to take back the area, but the California Republic insurgents held on until July 9, 1846, when the United States Marines landed in Monterey.

Bear Flag raised on June 14, 1846

The proclamation of the California Republic was however merely a sideshow in the war between Mexico and the United States. With the success of the American occupation, the Stars and Stripes flew over Sonoma.

The Mission Solano de Sonoma church was used as a parish church for the pueblo until 1881, while a new parish church separate from the mission grounds was built with funds from the sale of the mission properties. The new mission owner, Solomon Schocken, used the chapel and the priests' quarters to store wine and hay. Later, the quarters were used as a barn, chicken coop, and blacksmith shop. The California Historic Landmarks League, with William Randolph Hearst as its trustee, purchased the Solano Mission for $3,000 in 1903 with the intention of restoring it.

The mission became a California State Park in 1906, and was then partially restored between 1911 and 1913, thanks to a $5,000 state legislature appropriation. Mission San Francisco Solano de Sonoma opened as a museum on June 14, 1914, and in 1926 it was designated as California State Landmark No. 3. The original padres' quarters still stand, and the building constitutes the oldest structure in Sonoma.

Epilogue

A diminutive man, with the most powerful nation of the world behind him, changed the course of history, profoundly affecting government, education, and religion in the New World. Father Junípero Serra, a Franciscan who personified the ideals of St. Francis—humility, kindness, self-sacrifice, and generosity—envisioned a chain of missions that would span the length of California. In doing so, not only would he fulfill the desires of King Charles III of Spain to colonize the New World, but he also would civilize and Christianize the Native American population.

This dual purpose—colonization to protect Spain's holdings from the aspirations of other countries and the Christianization of the Indians—would strengthen Spain's position as a world power and fulfill Father Serra's calling.

The influence of the missions peaked during the era of Spanish rule, and waned for many decades thereafter. But the missions have again become a prominent force in shaping the culture and personality of California.

The impact of the early California missionary pioneers continues to resonate centuries later. Cities and streets are named after them, their statues are in parks and churches, their architecture influences our homes and businesses, and their history is studied in public schools. Visitors flock by the thousands to visit and immerse themselves in the lives and times of these long-ago residents of California.

Two centuries later, Father Junípero Serra and the California missions continue to educate and inspire us, as we ponder these monuments to faith and the people who took a wilderness and started it on the path that leads us to today.

Glossary

Adobe: clay and straw mixture used to make sun-dried brick

Alcalde: mayor of a Spanish-Portuguese or Spanish-American town

Aqueduct: a long channel or elevated bridge-like structure used for channeling water over a distance

Alta California: Upper California (became the state of California in the United States)

Arbor: a shady recess in a garden, with a canopy of trees or climbing plants

Arcade: an outside corridor

Asistencia: a sub-mission or annex to the main mission

Baja California: Lower California (became the state of Baja in Mexico)

Baptism: the Christian rite of sprinkling a person with water or immersing them in it, symbolizing purification and admission to the Christian Church

Baptistry: a building or part of a church used for baptisms

Baroque: a style of art, sculpture, architecture, and music of late 16th and 17th centuries

Barracks: large building to house soldiers

Barrel Organ: a small pipe organ that plays a preset tune when a handle is turned

Basilica: a Christian church; Latin for royal palace of historic importance, given special ceremonial privileges

Belfry: the place in a bell tower in which bells are housed

Brea: Spanish for tar or pitch

Buttress: a projecting support built against a wall

Campanario: an outer wall with openings for bells

Campanile: a belfry or bell tower

Candelabra: a large branched candlestick or holder for several candles

Capitals: the top part of a pillar or column

Cistern: a water storage tank; an underground reservoir for rainwater

Claretians: a religious group associated with the philosophy of St. Clare

Colonnade: an evenly spaced line of columns supporting an entablature

Colony: a country or area under the control of another country and occupied by settlers from that country

Colonize: establish a colony in (a place); take over (a place) for one's own use.

Convent: religious community, especially that of nuns; the establishment in which they live

Convento: priests' housing

Cornerstone: a stone that forms the base of a corner of a building, joining two walls

Cruciform: having the shape of a cross

Cupola: a rounded dome forming or adorning a roof or ceiling

Doric: resembling one of the classic orders of Greek architecture characterized by pillars having no ornament on their capitals

Dormitory: a bedroom for a number of people in an institution

Ecclesiastic: pertaining to the church

Emancipate: set free; especially from legal, social, or political restrictions

Encroach: gradually intrude on (a person's territory, rights, etc.)

Entablature: In classical architecture, the elaborated beam member, carried by the columns, horizontally divided into the architecture, frieze, and cornice

Epidemic: a widespread occurrence of an infectious disease in a community at a particular time

Evangelization: concerned with or relating to the preaching of the Christian gospel

Expedition: a journey undertaken by a group of people with a particular purpose

Façade: [fachada] the face of a building, especially the front

Fault: an extended break in a rock formation, marked by the relative displacement and discontinuity of strata

Foundry: a workshop or factory for casting metal

Font: a receptacle in a church for the water used in baptism

Fortress: a military stronghold, especially a strongly fortified town fit for a large garrison

Franciscan: one who follows the philosophy of St. Francis

Free-standing: not attached to or supported by another structure

Fresco: method of painting art on plaster by laying on the cover before the plaster is dry

Friar: a member of any of certain religious orders of men, especially the four mendicant orders: Augustinians, Carmelites, Dominicans, and Franciscans

Gargoyle: a grotesquely carved human or animal face or figure projecting from the gutter of a building, usually as a spout to carry water clear of a wall

Garland: a wreath of flowers and leaves, worn on the head or hung as a decoration

Garrison: a body of troops stationed in a fortress or town to defend it

Granary: a storehouse for threshed grain

Gristmill: a mill for grinding grain

Hostilities: antagonism; a hostile state between adversaries

Infirmary: a hospital or place set aside for the care of the sick or injured

Jesuit: a member of the Society of Jesus, a Roman Catholic order of priests founded by St. Ignatius Loyola and others in 1534

Jurisdiction: the official power to make legal decisions and judgment

Kiln: a furnace or oven for burning or baking, especially one for firing pottery

Lavanderia: an open-air stone laundry area

Limestone: a hard sedimentary rock composed mainly of calcium carbonate

Manuscript: a handwritten book, document, or piece of music; a text submitted for printing and publication

Mass: the Christian Eucharist or Holy Communion, especially as practiced in the Roman Catholic Church

Massacre: the brutal slaughter of a large number of people

Majordomo: chief steward in an Italian or Spanish household

Mendicant: of a religious order originally dependent on alms

Mezcla: mortar

Missal: a book of the texts used in the Catholic Mass

Missionary: a person sent on a religious mission

Monastery: a community of monks living under religious vows

Monk: a man belonging to a religious community and typically living under vows of poverty, chastity, and obedience

Moorish Architecture: The Islamic architecture of North Africa and of the regions of Spain under Islamic domination

Mortar: a mixture of lime with cement, sand, and water, used to bond bricks or stones

Mural: a painting executed directly upon a wall

Nave: the central part of a church apart from the side aisles, chancel, and transepts

Neophyte: a novice in a religious order, or a newly ordained priest

Nun: a member of a female religious community, typically one living under vows of poverty, chastity, and obedience

Octagon: a plain figure with eight straight sides and eight angles

Occupation: the action, or fact, of occupying a place

Padre: Spanish for father; in the California missions, a Franciscan missionary

Pagan: a person holding religious beliefs other than those of the main world religions

Pageantry: an elaborate display or ceremony

Parish: (in the Christian Church) a small administrative district with its own church and clergy

Peninsula: a long, narrow piece of land projecting out into a sea or lake

Philanthropy: the desire to help others, especially by donating money to good causes

Philosophy: the theories of a particular philosopher; a theory or attitude that guides one's behavior

Pilaster: a flat, vertical support usually used as a decoration

Pillar: a tall, vertical structure used as a support for a building or as an ornament

Plague: a contagious disease spread by bacteria and characterized by fever and delirium

Plaza: a public square or similar open space in a built-up area

Plunder: enter forcibly and steal goods from, especially during war or civil disorder

Politico: a politician or person with strong political views

Presidio: a large Spanish military fort used to house soldiers who protected the mission lands

Primitive: an extremely basic level of comfort, culture, or convenience

Province: a principal administrative division of a country or empire

Pueblo: a town or village in Spain, Latin America, or the southwestern United States, especially an American Indian settlement

Quadrangle: a four-sided geometrical figure, especially a square or rectangle; a square or rectangular courtyard enclosed by buildings

Ranchero: Spanish for rancher

Reredos: an ornamental screen at the back of an altar in a church

Replica: an exact copy or model of something, especially one on a smaller scale

Republic: a state in which supreme power is held by the people and their elected representatives, and which has an elected or nominated president rather than a monarch

Reservoir: a large natural or artificial lake used as a source of water supply; a receptacle or part of a machine designed to hold fluid

Rheumatism: any disease marked by inflammation and pain in the joints, muscles, or fibrous tissue, especially rheumatoid arthritis

Ruin(s): building(s), or remains of buildings, that have suffered much damage

Sandstone: sedimentary rock consisting of sand or quartz grains cemented together, typically red, yellow, or brown in color

Sanitarium: an establishment for the care of convalescent or chronically ill people

Scurvy: a disease caused by a deficiency of vitamin C, characterized by bleeding gums and the opening of previously healed wounds

Secular: not religious, sacred, or spiritual

Secularization Act of 1833: legally removing the missions from the authority of the priests and creating pueblos. The land was to be returned to the Indians, although secularization typically resulted in private ownership.

Seize: take forcible possession of; take possession of by warrant or legal right

Seminary: a training college for priests or rabbis

Serape: shawl or blanket worn as a cloak by people from Latin America

Shale: soft, stratified sedimentary rock formed from consolidated mud or clay

Sovereign: a king or queen who is the supreme ruler of a country

Syndic: an official, especially one who manages the business matters of a university or other corporation

Swallow: a swift flying migratory songbird with a forked tail, which feeds on insects in flight

Tallow: a hard fatty substance made from rendered animal fat, used in making candles and soap

Tannery: a place where hides are tanned

Terrain: a stretch of land, especially in regard to its physical features

Thatch: a roof covering of straw, reeds, or similar material

Transept: in a cross-shaped church, either of the two parts forming the arms of the cross shape, projecting at right angles from the nave

Transparent: allowing light to pass through so that objects behind can be distinctly seen

Trough: a long, narrow, open container for animals to eat or drink from; a channel used to convey a liquid

Vat: a large tank used to hold liquid

Vatican: the palace and official residence of the Pope in Rome

Vault: a roof in the form of an arch or a series of arches; a large room or chamber used for storage, especially underground; a chamber beneath a church or in a graveyard used for burials

Vestibule: an antechamber or hall just inside the outer door of a building

Vestment: a liturgical garment worn by a priest during an act of worship

Viceroy: a ruler exercising authority in a colony on behalf of a sovereign

Viol: a musical instrument of the Renaissance and Baroque periods, typically six-stringed, held vertically and played with a bow

Bibliography

Books

Adams, Kenneth C. *California Missions.* Los Angeles, California: California Missions Trails Assn., Ltd. 1947.

Alexander, James B. *Sonoma Valley Legacy.* Sonoma, California: Sonoma Valley Historical Society, 1986.

Boule, Mary Null. *The Missions: California's Heritage Mission Nuestra Señora de La Soledad.* Vashon, Washington: Merryant Publishers, Inc., 1988.

Boule, Mary Null. *The Missions: California's Heritage Mission San Francisco Solano.* Vashon, Washington: Merryant Publishers, Inc., 1988.

Boule, Mary Null. *The Missions: California's Heritage Mission San Rafael Arcangel.* Vashon, Washington: Merryant Publishers, Inc., 1988.

Boule, Mary Null. *The Missions: California's Heritage Mission San Francisco Solano.* Vashon, Washington: Merryant Publishers, Inc., 1988.

Boule, Mary Null. *The Missions: California's Heritage Mission Santa Cruz.* Vashon, Washington: Merryant Publishers, Inc., 1988.

Bowen, Robert W. *San Francisco's Presidio.* San Francisco, California: Arcadia Publishing, 2005.

Bruton, Lydian. *The Swallows of San Juan Capistrano.* Orange, California: The Paragon Agency, 2000.

Cleary, Br. Guire S.S.F. *Mission Dolores: The Gift of St. Francis.* Orange, California: The Paragon Agency, 2004.

Clough, Charles W. *San Juan Bautista.* Sanger, California: Word Dancer Press, 2006.

Engelhardt, Fr. Zephyrin, O. F. M. *Mission La Concepción Purísima de Maria Santisima.* Santa Barbara, California: McNally & Loftin Publishers, 1986.

Engelhardt, Fr. Zephyrin, O.F.M. *The Missions and Missionaries of California, Vol. III: Upper California.* San Francisco, California: The James H. Barry Company, 1913.

Engelhardt, Fr. Zephyrin, O.F.M. *The Missions of California, Vol. IV: Upper California.* San Francisco, California: The James H. Barry Company, 1915.

Engelhardt, Fr. Zephyrin, O.F.M. *The Missions and Missionaries of California: San Juan Capistrano Mission.* Los Angeles, California: 1922.

Engelhardt, Fr. Zephyrin O.F.M. *Missions and Missionaries of California: San Miguel Arcángel, The Mission on the Highway.* Santa Barbara, California: Mission Santa Barbara, 1929.

Engelhardt, Fr. Zephyrin, O.F.M. *The Missions and Missionaries of California: San Francisco or Mission Dolores.* Chicago, Illinois: Franciscan Herald Press, 1924.

Foster, Lee. *The Beautiful California Missions.* Wilsonville, Oregon: Beautiful America Publishing Company, 1986.

Gunthorp, Maude Robson. *With A Sketch Book Along the Old Mission Trail.* Caldwell, Idaho: The Caxton Printers, Ltd. 1940.

Hunter, Alexander. *Vallejo, A California Legend.* Sonoma, California: Sonoma State Historic Park Association, Inc. 1992.

Johnson, Paul C., et al. *The California Missions, A Pictorial History.* Menlo Park, California: Lane Book Company, 1974.

Kennedy, Roger G. *The History and Architecture of The Missions of North America.* New York: Houghton Mifflin Company, 1993.

Leffingwell, Randy, and Worden, Alastair. *California Missions and Presidios.* St. Paul, Minnesota: Voyageur Press, an imprint of MBI Publishing Company, 2005.

McKowen, Dahlynn, and Ken McKowen. *Best of California's Missions, Mansions and Museums.* Berkeley, California: Wilderness Press, 2007.

McLaughlin, David J. *Soldiers, Scoundrels, Poets & Priests.* Scottsdale, Arizona: Pentacle Press, 2004.

MacMillan, Dianne M. *Los Angeles Area Missions.* Minneapolis, Minnesota: Lerner Publications Company, 2008.

Miller, Henry. *Account of a Tour of The California Missions and Towns 1856.* Santa Barbara, California: Bellerophon Books, 2000.

Neuerburg, Norman. *Saints of the California Missions.* Santa Barbara, California: Bellerophon Books, 2001.

Neuerburg, Norman. *The Architecture of Mission La Purísima.* Santa Barbara, California: Bellerophon Books, 1987.

Newcomb, Rexford, M.Z., M. Arch., A.I.A. *The Old Mission Churches and Historic Houses of California.* Philadelphia & London: J.B. Lippincott Company, 1925.

Orser, Mary Beth. *A History of Soledad and the Surrounding Areas.* King City, California: Community Action Team of Soledad, 1996.

Osborne, James. *Missions of Southern California, Post Card History Series.* San Francisco, California: Arcadia Publishing, 2007.

Perouse, Jean Francois de La. *Life in a California Mission.* Berkeley, California: Heyday Books, 1989.

Salcedo-Chourre, Tracy. *A Falcon Guide to California's Missions and Presidios.* Guilford, Connecticut: The Globe Pequot Press, 2005.

Saones, Catherine, editor. *The Oxford Compact English Dictionary.* Oxford, UK: Oxford University Press, 2003

Selfridge, Vernon. *The Miracle Missions.* Los Angeles, California: Grafton Publishing Corporation, 1915.

The California Mission Story. Printed in China: Scenic Art, 1979.

Tibesar, Antonine, O.F.M., editor. *Diary by Serra of the Expedition from Loreto to San Diego March 28 to July 1, 1769.* Berkeley, California: Academy of American Franciscan History, 2007.

Weber, Msgr. Francis J. *A History of the Archdiocese of Los Angeles.* France, Editions du Signe, 2006.

Weber, Msgr. Francis J. *Blessed Fray Junípero Serra, An Outstanding California Hero.* San Fernando, California: San Fernando Mission, September, 2007.

Weber, Msgr. Francis J. *The California Missions.* Strasbourg, France: Editions du Signe, 2007.

Womack, Randy L. M., editor. *The Best Ever Book About California Missions.* Redding, California: Golden Educational Center, 2007.

Wood, Raymund F. *A Brief History of Mission San Jose.* Fresno, California: Academy Library Guild, 1957

Periodicals

Ambrosio, Katie. *Mission San Carlos Borromeo.* Carmel, California: John Hinde Curteich, 2000.

Carillo, Father J. M. *The Story of Mission San Antonio de Pala.* Oceanside, California: Fr. J. M. Carillo, 2006.

Case, Thomas, Dr. *Mission San Diego de Alcalá: The Origins of San Diego's Patron Saint Didacus of Alcalá.* San Diego, California: Occasional Papers Number I Presented by The Editorial Board Mission San Diego de Alcala, date unknown.

Dillon, Richard. *California Bicentennial Series No. 42.* San Diego, California: Standard Oil Company of California, Neyenesch Printers, Inc. 1969.

Eagen, I. Brent. *A History of Mission Basilica San Diego de Alcalá.* Brochure design, William Noonen, date unknown.

Geiger, Maynard, O.F.M., Ph.d. *Father Junípero Serra Paintings.* Santa Barbara, California: Franciscan Fathers, reprinted 1958.

Geiger, Maynard, O.F.M. Ph. D. *The Indians of Mission Santa Barbara in Paganism and Christianity.* Santa Barbara, California: Franciscan Fathers and the Serra Shop, Old Mission Santa Barbara, 1986.

Geiger, Maynard, O. F. M., PhD. *Mission Santa Bárbara: Queen of the Missions.* Santa Barbara, California: Old Mission Santa Barbara, date unknown.

Haas, Capistran J. O. F. M. *Saint Barbara: Her Story.* Santa Barbara, California: Old Mission Santa Barbara, 1988.

Kammerer, Raymond C. *Old Mission San Juan Capistrano.* Cincinnati, Ohio: KM Publications, 1981.

Kelsey, Harry. *Mission San Luis Rey.* Oceanside, California: Liber Apertus Press, 1993.

Leano Maria. "Preserving Historic and Spiritual Integrity," *Diocesan News*, Orange County Catholic, October, 2008.

Mission Santa Bárbara. Santa Barbara, California: Serra Shop, Old Mission Santa Barbara, date unknown.

Mylar, Isaac, L. *Early Days at the Mission San Juan Bautista.* Watsonville, California: Evening Pajaronian, 1919; reprint Word Dancer Press, Fresno, California, 1994.

Nolte, Carl. "Crumbling Away." San Francisco, California: *San Francisco Chronicle*, July 12, 2000.

O'Sullivan, St. John. *Little Chapters About San Juan Capistrano.* California: St. John O'Sullivan, 1912, reprinted Orange, California: The Paragon Agency, 1998.

Reese, Jennifer. "California Missions Saving Grace." San Francisco, California: *Via Magazine*, November/December 2005.

Mission Brochures and Pamphlets

Bob Hope Memorial Garden, author unknown. The Archdiocese of Los Angeles and Cardinal Roger Mahony, date unknown.

La Purisima Mission State Historic Park Self-Guided Tour. Lompoc, California: La Purisima Mission State Historic Park, date unknown.

Mission Basilica San Diego de Alcala, publisher and date unknown.

Mission Nuestra Senora de la Soledad, publisher and date unknown.

Mission San Francisco de Asís: "Welcome to Mission San Francisco de Asís, Popularly Known as Mission Dolores," publisher and date unknown.

Mission San Gabriel Arcangel, A Commemorative Edition. San Gabriel, California: Photografx Worldwide, LLC. California, 2008.

Mission San Gabriel Arcángel Pride of the California Missions. San Gabriel, California: San Gabriel Mission Museum and Gift Shop, 2008.

Mission San Juan Capistrano, author unknown. Oxnard, California: published by John Hinde Curteich, Inc., date unknown.

Mission San Juan Bautista. Lowman, Robert, based in part on text compiled by Martha H. Lowman. Arroyo Grande, California: Lowman Publishing Company, 2008.

Mission San Juan Capistrano, author unknown. Oxnard, California: published by John Hinde Curteich, Inc., date unknown.

Mission San Miguel Arcángel, publisher and date unknown.

Mission Santa Barbara. Santa Barbara, California: Old Mission Santa Barbara, date unknown.

Mission Santa Cruz, author unknown. Santa Cruz, California: Santa Cruz Mission State Historic Park, date unknown.

Mission Vieja, La Purisima Mission State Historic Park. Lompoc, California, publisher and date unknown.

Old Mission San Juan Bautista, publisher and date unknown.

San Carlos Borromeo de Monterey "Royal Presidio Chapel" San Carlos Cathedral, publisher and date unknown.

Santa Cruz Mission State Historic Park, California State Parks, date unknown.

Sonoma State Historic Park, California State Parks, 2002.

The Basilica of Mission San Carlos Borromeo del Rio Carmelo, date unknown.

Weber, Msgr. Francis J. *Mission San Fernando,* 1998.

Miscellaneous

DVD: Bolton, David, and Gay, Kathy. *Inside the California Missions.* Santa Barbara, California: Cultural Videos Documentary, 2006.

Power Point Presentation: *Golden Era of the 21 Missions.* Native Daughters of the Golden West, San Francisco, California, date unknown.

Electronic Sources

A Man's Quest Reverberates Up and Down State. Pool, Bob. LA Times [online, consulted September, 2009] Available on the World Wide Web: http://www.latimes.com/news/local/la-me-bells24.story (1of 3)12/27/2004 11:34-35 AM

Archaeological, Conservation and Preservation Projects at California Missions and Other Hispanic Sites. California Mission Studies Association [online, consulted December, 2008] Available on the World Wide Web: http://www.ca_missions.org/arch.html

A Virtual Tour of the California Missions El Camino Reál, [online, consulted September, 2009] Available on the World Wide Web: http://missiontour.org/related/elcaminoreal.htm

A Virtual Tour of the California Missions Santa Margarita de Cortona, [online, consulted September, 2009] Available on the World Wide Web: http://missiontour.org/sanluisobispo/santamargarita.htm

A Virtual Tour of the California Missions Santa Ysabel Asistencia, [online, consulted September, 2009] Available on the World Wide Web: http://missiontour.org/sandiego/asistencia.htm

Bell Timeline in Sketchy California Context, [online, consulted September, 2009] Available on the World Wide Web: http://www.bell.k12.ca.us/decades/history/timeline.htm

California History "The First Yankee Don," [online, consulted September, 2009] Available on the World Wide Web: http://www.cagenweb.com/archives/HistoricalRecords/First YankeeDon.htm

California Missions Foundation—Mission San Gabriel, Arcángel, [online, consulted March, 2009] Available on the World Wide Web: http://missionsofCalifornia.org/missions/mission04.html

California Mission History: San Carlos Borromeo de Carmelo, [online, Consulted February, 2009] Available on the World Wide Web: http://www.californiamissions.com/cahistory/sancarlos.html

California Missions—Secularization of the Missions, (Originally published early 1922), author unknown, [online, consulted September, 2009] Available on the World Wide Web: http://www.oldandsold.com/articles17/california-missions-5.shtml

California State Parks, Santa Cruz Mission State Historic Park, [online, consulted September, 2009] Available on the World Wide Web: http://www.parks.ca.gov/default.asp?page_id=548

El Camino Reál A Virtual Tour of the California Missions, [online, consulted May, 2009] Available on the World Wide Web: http://missiontour.org/related/elcaminoreal.htm

El Camino Reál Bell Dedicated, author unknown, [online, consulted September, 2009] Available on the World Wide Web: http://www.laprensasandiego.org/archive/june26/bell.htm

Gaspar de Portola San Diego Biographies. San Diego Historical Society, [online, consulted September, 2009] Available on the World Wide Web: http://www.sandiegohistory.org/bio/portola/portola.htm

Historic Mission San Jose, [online, consulted March, 2009] Available on the World Wide Web: http://www.missionsanjose.org/history.html

History of Prostitution in Santa Cruz, [online, consulted September, 2009] Available on the World Wide Web: http://researchforum.santacruzmah.org/viewtopic.php?t=152

In Search of the San Juan Bautista Mission Escolta. California State Parks, [online, consulted September, 2009] Available on the World Wide Web: http//www.parks.ca.gov/?page_id=24056

Is There any Specific Reason Why Mission San Carlos has 9 Bells. California Missions Resource Center, [online, consulted September, 2009] Available on the World Wide Web: http://www.missionscalifornia.com/are/there-any-specific-reason-why-mission-san-carlos-h...

Landmark 59—San Diego Presidio Site California State Historic Landmark 59, [online, consulted December, 2008] Available on the World Wide Web: http://www.donaldlaird.com/landmarks/counties/000-099/059.html

Landmark 79—Presidio of San Francisco, [online, consulted December, 2008] Available on the World Wide Web: http://www.donaldlaird.com/landmarks/counties/000-099/079.html

Landmark 316—Presidio of Sonoma, [consulted, December, 2008] Available on the World Wide Web: http://www.donaldlaird.com/landmarks/counties/300-399/316.html

Landmark 636—Royal Spanish Presidio California State Historic Landmark 636, [online, consulted December, 2008] Available on the World Wide Web: http://www.donaldlaird.com/landmarks/counties/600-699/636.html

Makers of the El Camino Reál Bell and Mission and Church Bells for Highway 101, [online, consulted September, 2009] Available on the World Wide Web: http://www.californiabell.com/

Mission Bells on Highway 101, editor, Los Angeles Almanac, [online, consulted September, 2009] Available on the World Wide Web: http://www.laalmanac.com/transport/tr32.htm

Mission Santa Cruz, [online, consulted September, 2009] Available on the World Wide Web: http://athanasius.com/camission/cruz.htm

Mission San Carlos Borromeo de Carmelo "Carmel Mission," [online, consulted September, 2009] Available on the World Wide Web: http://www.letsgoseeit.com/index/county/monterey/carmel/loc01/missionCarmel.htm

Mission San Fernando Rey de Espana, [online, consulted September, 2009] Available on the World Wide Web: http://www.missionart.com/hSFR/p-SFR.html

Mission San Jose, [online, consulted March, 2009] Available on the World Wide Web: http://www.athanasius.com/camission/san_jose.htm

Mission San Luis Obispo de Tolosa Mission San Luis Obispo: History. [online, consulted September, 2009] Available on the World Wide Web: http://missionsanluisobispo.org/history.html

Mission Trail Today. Larson, Kenneth A. [online, consulted September, 2009] Available on the World Wide Web: http://www.missiontrailtoday.com/code/mission_ae.htm

Monterey's First Years: The Royal Presidio of San Carlos de Monterey. Breschini, Gary S. Ph.D. [online, consulted September, 2009] Available on the World Wide Web: http://www.mchsmuseum.com/presidio.html

Old Mission Santa Ines Treasures of Mission Santa Ines, [online, consulted September, 2009] Available on the World Wide Web: http://missionssantaines.org/treasures.html

Panama-California Exposition - San Diego - 1915–1916. Bowers, J.D. [online, consulted September, 2009] Available on the World Wide Web: www.publichistory.org/reviews/View_Review.asp?DBID=96

Poverty and Wealth: Franciscan Dilemma in the Alta California of 1769–1835. Cleary, Brother Guire, S.S.F. [online, consulted December, 2008] Available on the World Wide Web: http://www.ca- missions.org/cleary.html

Roman Catholic Religious Order, [online, consulted November, 2008] Available on the World Wide Web: http://en.wikipedia.org/wiki/Roman_Catholic_religious_order

Saga of the Bells Comes Full Circle. Pool, Bob, Times Staff Writer, [online, consulted May, 2009] Available on the World Wide Web: http://californiabell.com/latimescentennial

San Carlos Cathedral (Royal Presidio Chapel) Monterey County Historical Society, [online, consulted September, 2009] Available on the World Wide Web: http://www.mchsmuseum.com/sancarlos.html

San Fernando Mission. Malloy, Betsy, About.com, [online, consulted September, 2009] Available on the World Wide Web: http://gocalifornia.about.com/cs/missioncalifornia/a/fernandohist.htm

San Gabriel Mission Church, [online, consulted September, 2009] Available on the World Wide Web: http://sangabrielmission.org/about/mission-church/

Santa Clara de Asís, More California Mission History, [online, consulted September, 2009] Available on the World Wide Web: http://www.californiamissions.com/morehistory/santaclara.html

Serra's San Diego. Engstrand, Iris H.W. [online, consulted September, 2009] Available on the World Wide Web: http://www.sandiegohistory.org/book/ssd/ssd.htm

Sonoma Mission Exterior, [online, consulted September, 2009] Available on the World Wide Web: http://missiontour.org/sonoma/tour04.htm

The El Camino Reál and Its Historic Bells, author unknown, California Bell Company. *Los Angeles Times,* [online, consulted May, 2009] Available on the World Wide Web: http://www.californiabell.com

The Journal of San Diego History. Bevil, Alexander D. [online, consulted September, 2009] Available on the World Wide Web: https://www.sandiegohistory.org.journal/92summer/mission.htm

The Old Spanish Trail—San Gabriel, California, [online, consulted March, 2009] Available on the World Wide Web: http://www.waymarking.com/waymarks/WM51H1

The Presidios of Alta California. California Mission Studies Assn. Articles. [online, consulted December, 2008] Available on the World Wide Web: http://www.ca-missions.org/honig.html

The San Bernardino Estancias. Harley R. Bruce, California Mission Studies Assn. Articles, [online, consulted September, 2009] Available on the World Wide Web: http://www.ca-missions.org/oldsite/harley.html

Villa Branciforte Preservation Society, [online, consulted September 2009] Available on the World Wide Web: http://www.villabranciforte.org/

Index